P9-CQX-800

TEACHING AND
RELIGIOUS IMAGINATION

Teaching and Religious Imagination

Maria Harris

1817

Harper & Row, Publishers, San Francisco

Cambridge, Hagerstown, New York, Philadelphia, Washington
London, Mexico City, São Paulo, Singapore, Sydney

Acknowledgments can be found on page 203.

TEACHING AND RELIGIOUS IMAGINATION. Copyright © 1987 by Maria Harris. All rights reserved. Printed in the United States of America. No part of this book may be used or reproduced in any manner whatsoever without written permission except in the case of brief quotations embodied in critical articles and reviews. For information address Harper & Row, Publishers, Inc., 10 East 53rd Street, New York, NY 10022. Published simultaneously in Canada by Fitzhenry & Whiteside, Limited, Toronto.

FIRST EDITION

Library of Congress Cataloging-in-Publication Data

Harris, Maria.
    Teaching and religious imagination.

    Bibliography: p.
    Includes index.
    1. Teaching—Religious aspects—Christianity.
    2. Imagination.   I. Title.
    LB1027.2.H37   1987   371.11′02   86-45381
    ISBN 0-06-254801-8

87 88 89 90 91 RRD 10 9 8 7 6 5 4 3 2 1

For Gabriel, beloved teacher

Contents

Preface

No book is ever written alone, and this one is no exception. It is the result of every teacher with whom I have worked, or with whom I have studied, or toward whom I have looked for clues to the meanings of teaching. It is the result of every teacher-student interaction I have had with literally thousands over the past thirty-five years: from my six-year-old music students in Bedford-Stuyvesant, Brooklyn, to my graduate students in Boston, New York, and Melbourne, Australia.

Still, certain persons stand out, and these must be named. I have stolen shamelessly from Margaret Woodward, and she will see her influence from beginning to end, especially in the citation of poets. I have learned enormously from colleagues who read the manuscript and commented on it, most especially John Westerhoff, Loretta Jancoski, Edward Robinson, Jack Priestley, David Steward, Regina Coll, Gwyn Griffith, Yvette Nelson, and Craig Dykstra. I have changed my own teaching and the ways I do it because of living with, working with, and observing Rosemary Crumlin. And I am able to offer readers an immensely better book because of the reverent and care-filled work of my editor, Jim Bitney.

But the three people to whom I owe most are those who have accompanied me on the journey of teaching almost from the beginning. Mary Tunny Harris was the first teacher I ever met (we met on my birth day), and throughout her teaching career I was profoundly influenced by how much she loved both her students and her teaching. Joanmarie Smith and I have been talking about teaching since we were teenagers; the most recent talk being the conversations we had as each chapter was completed. Those conversations were, quite simply, invaluable. And finally the teacher who changed my life, my understanding, my mind and heart, and my vocation: my husband, Gabriel Moran, to whom this book is dedicated. What he has taught me has become so much a part of myself that I find it difficult to distinguish his thought from mine.

To each of these persons, I offer my gratitude and my affection. They have incarnated subject matter in ways that have led me to revelation. They have enabled me to claim the grace of power. I hope I am true to them in this book where I attempt to re-create and re-render teaching, and in reading it I hope they will recognize something of the same beauty they first shared with me.

Introduction

One of the great sorrows in human life is the discovery, too late, of our own beauty and of the beauty of much that we do. Such is often the case with teachers, as we contemplate ourselves and our vocation. At the deepest level, every teacher wants to become a better teacher, even a great teacher; in moments of insight, every teacher is aware of hidden gifts of creativity and imagination. But often the pressures, deadlines, and exigencies of dailiness keep teachers from standing back and viewing their work with the care both they and their work deserve. Often when there might be time at faculty meetings or on in-service days, demands for the newest, the latest, and the updated can get in the way and preclude the possibility of standing back, of being still and recalling the excitement and lure which drew us to teaching in the first place. We need an arena, a context, and an occasion to contemplate our teaching and to recover, if we have lost them, the dreams and the hopes, the vision and the grandeur that lie at the core of teaching. We need an opportunity to rediscover the creative, artistic teachers we are and were meant to be.

My hope is that this book will provide such an arena. I have been working with teachers for three decades, but in the last few years my interest has increasingly been caught by teachers who want to preserve and conserve the dimension of beauty; the dimension of depth in their work. When they speak of teaching, more often than not their speech is in the realm of imagination; moreover, it is expressed as much if not more by experienced teachers who have been working at teaching for many years. Beginning teachers and temporary or volunteer teachers have the same hopes, but are many times preoccupied with survival or basic strategies, concerns often met through mastering techniques and procedures. In contrast, experienced teachers who have reached a level of competence often find themselves asking, "Is this all there is?" To my mind, that question indicates a movement toward rich, deep meaning. It signals the presence of a reflective person who has reached a point of choice: either to settle into a routine of humdrum and narrow boredom, or to be reborn into an imaginative educational world.[1] Unless new ways of understanding and addressing teaching are found, such teachers reach a point where their teaching becomes routinized, even stultifying.

I write as advocate for such teachers in the belief that much more can be offered and that teaching remains a magnificent challenge in a person's life. We need to go beyond speaking and writing, which address us at the survival and basic competence levels alone, the levels where we are simply learning to stay afloat. We need to be engaged even more—not less—once the initial difficulties of the new role or the new topic are resolved.[2] Allow me now to explore something of how I propose that engagement might be accomplished.

If we examine writing on teaching, we find what I refer to as *genres*. The first of the genres are books on techniques and procedures, the "how to teach" books. Many of these books have great value for beginners. However, since they can convey the impression that teaching is mainly a technical skill without conveying any broader vision, such books are often less helpful and even damaging to the imaginative and resourceful teacher.

A second genre of books, books of more value for the teachers who are my primary concern, are autobiographical accounts of teaching. I think, for example, of Sylvia Ashton-Warner's *Teacher*, her classic description of her work with Maori children in New Zealand, and her subsequent work, *Spearpoint: Teacher in America*. I think also of a number of books published in the United States in the 1960s: Jonathan Kozol's *Death at an Early Age*, John Holt's *How Children Fail*, and George Dennison's *The Lives of Children*. I recall Seonaid Robertson's accounts of teaching art to miners' children in Britain in *Rosegarden and Labyrinth*, of E. R. Braithwaite's *To Sir with Love*, Pat Conroy's *The Water Is Wide*, Esther Rothman's *The Angel Inside Went Sour*, and Richard Rodriguez's poignant memoir, *Hunger of Memory*.[3] Finally, I remember passages in Judy Chicago's *Through the Flower* and in Northrop

Frye's *The Great Code,* where both describe revealing moments in their own teaching.[4]

A third genre of books illuminates the nature of teaching through drama, novel, or the form of *bildungsroman,* the last being the story of a life seen as an entire education. In this genre we find several works of Herman Hesse: *Magister Ludi, Narcissus and Goldmund,* and *Siddhartha.*[5] Other books of this genre are May Sarton's lovely novel about the teacher Lucy Winter called *The Small Room,*[6] the classic *Goodbye Mr. Chips,*[7] and the instructive and sobering novel of Muriel Spark, *The Prime of Miss Jean Brodie.*[8] The genre also includes several plays: for example, *The Corn is Green, The Miracle Worker,* and *Pygmalion.*[9] Although this genre of books is easily as illuminating as textbooks about teaching, and generally far more so, such books and plays are absent from the regular curricula for teaching teachers about teaching. However, there is one textbook that does draw on such work: the superbly edited collection of Landau, Epstein, and Stone, *The Teaching Experience: An Introduction to Education Through Literature.*[10]

Finally, there is a fourth genre of books that deals with the philosophy of education: Gilbert Highet's *The Art of Teaching* is one;[11] Paulo Freire's *Pedagogy of the Oppressed,* and, perhaps even more, his *Education for Critical Consciousness* are two others.[12] Several works of R. S. Peters and John Dewey qualify,[13] as do Martin Buber's essay "Education," from *Between Man and Man*[14] and Alfred North Whitehead's essay "The Rhythm of Education," from *The Aims of Education.*[15] Much of Maria Montessori's work fits into this genre as well.[16] In all of this work, however, I wish to distinguish between that which deals with philosophy of education as a whole, which includes a broad range of concerns, and that which deals with the more specific philosophy of *teaching.*

Although this book is written mostly in the areas of theology and philosophy, I have tried to work in a way that cuts across and interrelates all four genres. With reference to techniques and procedures, I use examples throughout the work but especially in chapters 3, 7, 8, and 9 of specific things teachers might do and actually have done in teaching situations. I have also been autobiographical throughout, alluding to my own experience as illustrative, and giving an extended and direct account in chapter 8. In chapter 7, I describe a great teacher—a worthy subject for a novel—at work. But mainly, I have tried to offer a reflective, phenomenological, philosophical essay on the nature of teaching.

My vision throughout will be focused on teaching, rather than moving to curricular, institutional, and supervisory issues. I believe that books on teaching in actuality often become books on schools, supervision, curriculum, and psychology of learning without giving adequate attention to the teaching activity itself. Underlying such books' swift shift of vision appears to be the assumption that "everyone knows" what is involved in teaching. I take sharp issue with this assumption. Everyone does *not* know what is involved, and far more attention must be given to conversation about, to dwelling in, and to sitting with the teaching act itself.

The particular contribution I hope to make is to examine the ways in which religion and imagination might be brought to bear upon teaching. More specifically, I want to bring religion and imagination together under the rubric of religious imagination, in ways related to but distinct from Elliot Eisner's bringing art and imagination together.[17] To do this I use the following format.

Part I, the book's main section, consists of six chapters. In chapter 1, "Imagination and the Religious," I will clarify my use of the book's three central terms: *religion, imagination,* and *religious imagination.* Chapter 2 moves to teaching itself and offers a paradigm for teaching, looking at it religiously and imaginatively rather than technically or psychologically. This teaching paradigm is based on working with clay and should be a process familiar to potters, sculptors, and other artistic creators.

Chapters 3, 4, 5, and 6 discuss four religious metaphors, using each as an interpretive key for understanding the nature of teaching as an act of religious imagination. The metaphors are *incarnation, revelation, power,* and *re-creation.* Chapter 3 ("Incarnation") is a study of how the religiously imaginative teacher incarnates form—makes subject matter incarnate—in the movement toward knowledge and wisdom. Chapter 4 ("Revelation") follows from this incarnation, and draws on the mode of indirect communication associated with Sören Kierkegaard. Chapter 5, "The Grace of Power," attempts to describe and speculate on what the revelation of subject matter leads to: namely, human beings as subjects claiming their own capacities, abilities, and powers, which have been discovered through the activity of revelation. Finally, in chapter 6 ("Re-Creation"), I complete the phenomenology of teaching by suggesting that it issues in re-creation. I will also offer a second paradigm for teaching, akin to that in chapter 2. However, the distinction of the sixth chapter's paradigm is that it draws on the experience of the *outsider*, the *strange*, and the *stranger*, as essential to any understanding of teaching in our time. From these four chapters, the following thesis gradually emerges and becomes clarified:

Teaching, when seen as an activity of religious imagination, is the incarnation of subject matter in ways that lead to the revelation of subject matter. At the heart of this revelation is the discovery that human beings are the primary subjects of all teaching, subjects who discover themselves as possessing the grace of power, especially the power of re-creation, not only of themselves, but of the world in which they live.

Because this is a book about teaching, however, it would be incomplete without an attempt to provide exemplars or models— human models—of teaching. Thus, Part II is a shorter section containing three chapters. Chapter 7, "A Pedagogical Model," describes a genius teacher at work, the late Mary Anderson Tully of the faculty of Union Theological Seminary in New York City. She was this teacher's teacher. Chapter 8, "An Artistic Model," describes a course I have taught over the years, and illustrates one of the ways I work, the way of art. As such, it provides examples of the embodied form of teaching that incarnates through the aesthetic; at the same time, it provides a glimpse of the author at work as a teacher. The final chapter, "Invitation to Imagination," offers criteria and counsel to teachers in terms of developing their own imaginative capacities and their own teaching models.

If the book has originality and strength, and I am bold enough to believe that it has or I would not be writing, such strength lies in four elements. The first element of strength is the set of paradigms, found in chapters 2 and 6. The paradigm on teaching (chapter 2) is one I have explored over the last five years with hundreds of teachers, and is one those teachers have found resonant with their own lives. The second paradigm (chapter 6, "Re-Creation") outlines my dual assumption that the starting point of learning must be the experience of the "outsider" and that the beginning of all genuine wisdom is the acknowledgment of the thing that does not fit but which, if acknowledged, leads to reform and re-creation.

This paradigm drawn from the outsider leads to a second and necessary element of the book's strength: the compatibility of the outsider image with the experience of women throughout the world. As such, the paradigm represents the feminist orientation of the book. This orientation, as Jane Roland Martin has brilliantly shown in her essays on Rousseau and Pestalozzi, has been sadly absent from philosophy of education.[18]

The book's third claim to originality and strength lies in its movement to bring together two realms often separated from each other. The first is the realm of *imagination, religion,* and *art,* which draws on symbol and form, intuition and experience. The second is the realm of the *social* and *political,* the *corporate* and *communal,* often assumed to be distinct from the first. My claim here will be for the importance of both, and more, for both in interplay and intercourse with each other.

Finally, the book's fourth element of strength lies in its attempt to help practicing teachers speak philosophically and theoretically, but with concrete actuality, about their work. We practitioners are often thought of as mere technicians or as being so involved with people at the levels of ordinary dailiness that we do not stand back to reflect with seriousness on what we do. Often this leads to a charge that although we are strong in the heart, we are soft in the head.

I hope that charge will not be made of me, or of this book. I hope, instead, that it will be read and received as one teacher's attempt, out of the experience of many years, out of conversations with thousands of teachers, out of profound conviction about the importance of imagination and concern for the "deeper things," to record that experience and those conversations, to encourage that conviction, and to say to teachers who love their work: This is noble, beautiful, and graced activity, this teaching; a religious vocation, which, when entered into with grace and dwelt in with fidelity, has the power to re-create the world.

I. TEACHING

1. Imagination and the Religious

"It is possible, possible, possible. It must be possible."

WALLACE STEVENS

In his poem "Brief Thoughts on Maps," Miroslav Holub describes how a young Hungarian officer sends a detachment of his men into the Alps. No sooner have they left than heavy snow begins to fall. The landscape is blotted out. The men do not return. Frantic and guilt-ridden, the officer reproaches himself. His orders have condemned his men to death.

Three days later, however, the men come back. How can this be? How could they possibly find their way? Well, they admit, they did give up for a bit. Then one of them, reaching into a pocket, found a map. And so they waited out the storm. Then, using the map, they found their way back.

The officer borrowed this remarkable map and had a good look at it. To his surprise, he found it was not a map of the Alps, but of the Pyrenees![1] Because his troops had *imagined* the power to return home, because they had believed they had the capacity to survive, they made the impossible possible.

Imagination brought to bear on the act of teaching has a power similar to that map of the Pyrenees, a power which saves from death. The more I teach—and teach others to teach—the more I am convinced that the activity of teaching, when viewed as a religiously imaginative act, is able to save and to redeem. Although techniques and procedures and skills will always be needed for some understanding of teaching, these are not its heart. The heart of teaching is imagination, which, in Paul Ricoeur's words, "has a prospective and explorative function in regard to the inherent possibilities of human beings." For Ricoeur, "the imagination is par excellence, the instituting and constituting of what is humanly possible; in imagining possibilities, human beings act as prophets of their own existence."[2]

Ricoeur draws two conclusions: the first is that imagination

Forms of Religious Imagination

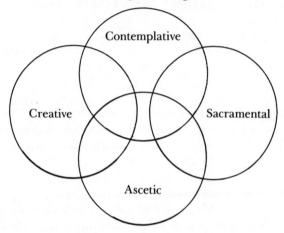

understood this way is redemptive; the second is that since every real conversion is first a revolution at the level of our directive images, we can alter our existence by changing our imaginations. The Pyrenees can become the Alps; death can give way to life; we can find our way home.

Reading Ricoeur, I am always struck by the religious quality of his language. Redemption, salvation, acting as prophets—these are religious terms. But I am also continually struck, due to my own angle of vision, by how applicable these words are to the work of teachers. For we teachers, at our best, can shape and reshape subject matter in order to present, to institute, and to constitute what is, has been, and might be humanly possible. Essential to the teaching role, then, is the work of creating possibilities, of handing on the belief that we have within us the capacity to alter our existence.

Chapter 2 is devoted to the act of teaching, and then we will go on to look at that act as one of religious imagination. In this first chapter, however, we will begin to probe some of the meanings—set out the grammar—of *imagination,* of *the religious,* and of *religious imagination;* for I will draw on these meanings throughout the rest of this book. I choose to qualify the word "meanings" with the adjective "some" for what I hope are obvious reasons. The three concepts—*imagination, the religious,* and *religious imagination*—are not amenable to easy definition; they have a plethora of associations, denotations, and connotations. Thus, I am wary of making any final or definitive statement to indicate one particular and essential meaning for any of the concepts. At the same time, however, I feel it is necessary for me to set out some initial rendering of those concepts, for they are essential to the argument of this book.

IMAGINATION: EMERGING MEANINGS

RECENT WRITING

The last several years have witnessed a remarkable burgeoning of interest in imagination, especially as it is related to the fields of philosophy, education, art, theology, and religious study. Works such as David Tracy's *The Analogical Imagination,* Elliot Eisner's *The Educational Imagination,* Lynn Ross Bryant's *Imagination and the Life of the Spirit,* John Dixon's *Art and Theological Imagination,* Ray Hart's *Unfinished Man and the Imagination,* and Walter Brueggemann's *The Prophetic Imagination* are symptomatic of this interest.[3] From one perspective, I am convinced that such interest expresses what W. H. Auden once spoke of as a "wild prayer of longing" resting at the core of the human spirit. The longing, expressed through a search for various interpretations and applications of imagination to life, is at least partly a reaction to a scientific and technical culture where the root metaphor of the times is the machine.[4] Hearts and spirits are experiencing the inadequacy and sterility that the technical conveys—in any field—when it is the dominant symbol of a culture. Thus, we are groping our way toward the creation of new images.

POLITICAL IMPULSES

From another perspective, the call to exercise imagination has been pressed by women and men long mired in oppressive and dehumanizing social contexts. Such people's hopes have been set afire not only by the prophets of the century, but by a stirring in their own bones: Rosa Parks, who imagined a different social order through long years in civil rights activity before finally refusing to give up her seat on a Montgomery, Alabama bus; the articulate and wise Martin Luther King, Jr., whose "I Have a Dream" speech is one of the quintessential imaginative statements of our time; poets Adrienne Rich and Marge Piercy, who look closely at the lives of women in our century: Rich seeing literature as "re-vision,"[5] Piercy writing that, although we do not have a past to share, we can work together and more: "We can love, we can love, we can love."[6] Beyond the borders of the United States, the works of the patriot poets Julia Esquivel and Ernesto Cardenal enflesh the hopes of the poorest; Nadine Gordimer and Athol Fugard offer images of South Africa's bruised world calling for global response; and educational philosopher Paulo Freire enables us not only to see, but to hear voices coming from people living in a culture of silence.[7]

SCIENTIFIC IMPULSES

New images also arise from the world of science. These images are of special importance to teachers, because they draw our attention to forms of knowing. Research in neuropsychiatry and the physiology of the brain suggests there is an extraordinary range to our knowing. Because of science, many are rediscovering intuitive, metaphorical, and symbolic knowledge. Biologists like Lewis Thomas, citing the interdependent nature of our physical bodies as humans with the physical bodies of nonhuman reality, bring poetry and medicine together in a disposition of imaginative awe.[8] Even more striking, the work of subatomic physicists suggests that scientists, artists, and mystics have something in common. In *The Tao of Physics*, Fritjof Capra notes that scientists who probe inside the atom can no longer rely on the forms of knowing of logic and common sense: "Physicists are now dealing with a nonsensory experience of reality and . . . face the paradoxical aspects of this experience."[9]

The common element found in these impulses, it seems to me, is the presence of imagination expressed in the call not only for more appropriate images and symbols, but, beyond that, for the kind of humane and humanizing social, economic, and political structures that can arise only from visionary work.

These women and men appear to share a common belief: imagination can change, reverse, and re-create present reality. What, then, is the nature of such power? What do we mean when we speak of imagination?

HISTORY: KANT AND COLERIDGE

A tendency exists in some to limit the meaning of imagination to fantasy or make-believe, even to assume it refers to a kind of nonserious dabbling or dilettantism of the mind. The last three hundred years, however, have done much to dissipate this tendency.[10] History itself has moved the human community to acknowledge the fundamental seriousness of imagination, indeed, to acknowledge the profound nature of this gift. In the West, the work of Keats, Blake, and Wordsworth did much to foster the recovery of imagination, seeing in the *idea* of it a reconciling, healing possibility for overcoming much of the dualism of the seventeenth century. Two other authors, Immanuel Kant and Samuel Taylor Coleridge, are especially significant in this anti-dualistic stance.

Kant's notion of imagination as *einbildungskraft,* the power of shaping into one, is often noted as a critical temporal point in the turn to and return to imagination. With this doctrine, Kant provided a grammar for understanding imagination.[11] Kant's preeminence as a philosopher provided a kind of respectability to an enterprise which, because of its links with art and feeling, was often in danger of dismissal, especially in the overly rational and rationalistic circles of the Enlightenment.

Coleridge brought a different, independent, yet companion vocabulary and grammar to the discussion on imagination. Coleridge gave us the language of primary and secondary imagination. For him, the primary imagination functions by actively fusing the fleeting impingements of sensation into a recognizable whole; the primary imagination is the imagination as active intelligence, reaching out in a primordial, preconscious enterprise of comparison and selective recognition.[12] Coleridge's insights enable us to become aware of the everydayness of imagination, its commonness, and its omnipresence. They also help us recognize, perhaps with something of a shock, that we are always involved in imagining, that imagination is always accessible to us, and that it is as natural and near as breath.[13] Imagination is not trivialized by its dailiness, for its correlative is that we are always creating, shaping, and constituting our worlds and our lives.

Coleridge also distinguished the secondary imagination: the more concrete activity employed in the poetic art.[14] The secondary imagination is the imagination as it dissolves and diffuses in order to re-create; the imagination embodied in music, myth, poetry, dance, and sculpture, giving us the great and refined forms of things unknown and unknowable through ordinary speech and discourse.

Coleridge was well aware that attempts to make distinctions, such as he was doing in speaking of primary and secondary imaginations, could lead to an overly intellectual and dangerously abstract conceptualization. Writing in 1797 on this point, he said:

I have known some who have been rationally educated as it is styled. They were marked by a microscopic acuteness but when they looked at great things, all became a blank and they saw nothing, and denied (very illogically) that anything could be seen, and uniformly put the negation of a power for the possession of a power and called the want of imagination judgment and the never being moved to rapture philosophy.[15]

CAVEATS

Coleridge's commentary on so-called rational education leads me to make several suggestions. The first is a counsel to avoid the serious mistake of being so careful in specifying the meaning of imagination that one loses its inherent ambiguity, its tendency to invite opposite evaluations. Imagination is far too complex a reality to be reduced to mere definition. It is imagination's nature *not* to pin down. Imagination keeps turning to reveal other facets, to bring intelligence to bear in such a way that enigma, irony, and paradox are often its fruits. We see something of this in the fact that imagination is essentially a faculty of the mind, and essentially a faculty of the body at the same time. Imagination takes these two, sometimes opposing elements of human nature and fuses into one *(einbildungskraft)* the intellectual, conceptual, and mental powers associated with the mind and the incarnational, corporeal, and physical capacities associated with the body. Imagination characteristically looks at reality from the reversed, unnoticed side; as such, it is the mind's glory, the ample fullness of intelligence, rather than the thinness of reason alone. At the same time, however, since imagination is always a human power, rooted in body and biography, it continually spills over the boundaries of mind so as to be always more comprehensive and comprehending. William Lynch can thus "define" imagination—and I would wish to join him— as "all the faculties of human beings, all our resources, not only our seeing and hearing and touching, but also our history, our education, our feelings, our wishes, our love, hate, faith and unfaith, insofar as they all go into the making of our image of the world."[16] The importance of this body/mind, reasoned/feeling character of imagination will become clearer in the course of this book as we examine the act of teaching and its relation to imagination. For the present, let me note that in terms of thought and mind, the teaching any of us do is affected, perhaps more than we realize, by the way we think about, conceptualize, and mentally picture our own teaching. At the same time, teaching is essentially an embodied, incarnate act carried on in a situation where human beings are physically present to one another. To draw on Lynch's notion, teaching is dependent on the total resources in us, our students, and our environments, all of which go into the making of *our* worlds.

THE GLOBAL ELEMENTS

Giving still more breadth to the meaning of imagination, a further insight comes from the famous plea of Yeats in his prayer for old age. Yeats reminds us not to understand imagination only through studying it in theory. "God save us from the thoughts men think/ In the mind alone,/ He that sings a lasting song/ Thinks in a marrow bone."[17] Much of the power in the rebirth of imagination today, especially its social force, comes from the wedding of thought *and* marrow bone; for example, from movements around the world that *are* passionate, that see everything (in contrast to seeing nothing and never being moved to rapture) as transformable, or as Stevens put it, "possible, possible, possible."

Today, imagination *is* theory, but it is *theory-and-more:* theory embodied in profound political, social action. Our times are characterized by the recognition that speculation is incomplete without attempted realization: Women are reclaiming images of divinity born from knowledge of Isis, Lilith, Demeter, Kali, and Mary; peasants and farmers are asserting birthright to their own lands; Hindu men and women are performing street theater in Calcutta to protest the burning of brides who bring no dowry; women and men of color are singing in the marrow bone, "We Shall Overcome"; peacemakers are singing, "Where are the bullets to buy back the dreams of the children who will never grow old?" Because of the power of imagination, we are acting as prophets of our own existence. We are in the process of becoming one race fleshing out dreams of reconciliation in a movement that cannot be stopped except by obliteration of the planet itself. If we would understand imagination fully, therefore, we need to study such movements and this, too, will have implications for teaching. Such movements will instruct us that our teaching is always a political act, whether we will it or not; that the nature of teaching is essentially social, located as it is in the midst of the body politic of this planet. Therefore, teaching can foster community and communion, or it can foster isolation and elitism. What it cannot do, in relation to the polis or to the environment in which it occurs, is be neutral.

THE RELIGIOUS AS PERSPECTIVE

The qualifier word I wish to offer in this book concerning the imagination is the word "religious." My central thesis is that teaching is an act not only of the imagination, but of the *religious* imagination. What does that mean? How, for example, is the religious imagination distinguished from the political imagination, the artistic imagination, the analogical imagination, or the educational imagination—all phrases one can easily find in contemporary thought? The notion of "valuing" provides a clue.

Several years ago, Dwayne Huebner raised for teachers the question of the range of valuing perspectives they used to reflect on their educational activity.[18] I am concerned that one of these perspectives be the religious one: A religious perspective is a way to value, to approach a human activity from a particular angle of vision, where the particularity leads to certain choices. The term "value" is particularly helpful in this regard, and I have intentionally chosen it over the more common educational term "evaluate." Where evaluating connotes an objectivity that allows the observer to stand back, appraise, and judge, valuing is at once a more personal, bodily word. Valuing carries with it a sense of subjective involvement and participation in what I, as a person, esteem or find desirable. In addition, valuing is an artist's word. In music, value/valuing signifies the duration of a tone or rest, in painting, the relative darkness or lightness of a color. The questions to which such allusions have always led me are whether valuing might be approached from a religious perspective, and if so, what ramifications this would have for teachers. Perhaps we can find some.

We tend to use many different lenses through which to examine human action, among them the scientific, the technical, the political, the psychological, and the aesthetic.[19] Valuing teaching as *scientific,* for instance, we might ask questions like the following: "If I do this, what will be the result?" or "What are the conditions necessary if this particular way of teaching is to achieve the ends I envision?" Valuing teaching as *technical,* we might ask a different, yet related set of questions: "What procedures do I use?" or "What steps do I follow?" or "Have I specified my goals and objectives clearly?" Valuing teaching from a *political* perspective, we come at the subject from yet another angle: "Where is the power in this situation?" or "To what social change might this mode of teaching contribute?" Valuing teaching as *psychological,* we would place great stress on the developmental capacities of students at particular ages, on readiness, on group processes as these affect the teaching activity, and on idiosyncratic personal differences. Indeed, in the format for studying teaching devised by Joyce and Weil, an entire family of models are based on psychological valuing.[20] Valuing teaching as *aesthetic,* we would be concerned with style, pace, design, rhythm, and shape in the activity of teaching, and with the human impulse toward form.

These different ways of valuing are not new to any of us, but I believe it is helpful to name them and to discover in the naming that our visions of teaching are affected in many ways by these particular ways of valuing. In addition, they are not discrete and often overlap or act as companions and partners to one another. For example, later in this book I will be drawing many connections between religious and political valuing and between religious and aesthetic valuing. Making distinctions between these ways of valuing now, however, fosters three important questions: (1) Is there a way of valuing—or, to use the language of imagination, a way of "seeing"—that could be called *religious?* (2) Can we specify characteristics of religious valuing? (3) Can religious valuing be brought to bear on the imagination in a way which enables us to speak of the "religious imagination"? I believe the answer to each of these questions is yes.

For centuries, wars have been fought on religious grounds. This fact indicates that no easy definition or meaning of the religious can easily satisfy human beings. However, it may be helpful to distinguish religion in the broader sense, from religion in the narrower sense. Paul Tillich describes religion in the broader sense as "being ultimately concerned about one's own being, about one's self and one's world, about its meaning and its estrangement and its finitude"; he describes religion in the narrower sense as our "having a set of symbols . . . divine beings . . . ritual actions and doctrinal formulations about their [divine beings'] relationship to us."[21] As a beginning foray into the meaning of religious, it is the broader meaning on which I draw, namely, the impulse toward what is of ultimate concern and meaning. At the same time, however, since none of us are religious in general, the narrower understanding of religion interpenetrates the broader and is never entirely absent from discussion of the religious. In the United States, where I live and work, this narrower understanding still draws largely from Jewish and Christian sources, although the influence of Eastern religions continues to grow here. In other words, it is possible to distinguish between broader and narrower senses of the religious, but not to separate the two. Since it is my goal to focus on questions of ultimacy and depth, however, I will be exploring the religious—as it applies to teaching—in its *broader* sense. I believe that such a focus will allow me to engage in *imaginative* activity, the sort of activity that is essential to any exploration where understandings of depth, ultimacy, and meaning are the primary considerations. In subsequent chapters, I shall draw more specifically on the tradition I know best, Christianity, especially its theology of incarnation and revelation; I will also draw on political theology, thus coming back to more specific understandings of the religious.

Different religious traditions bring different qualities of the religious to the fore. Nevertheless, certain qualities tend to be present in the religious self-understandings of most people. The qualities I wish to highlight are *mystery*, the *numinous*, and the *mystical*.

MYSTERY

A mystery is not that about which we cannot know anything, but that about which we cannot know everything. Gabriel Marcel has given us a famous and illuminating distinction between mystery and problem. A problem is something I meet that bars my passage and that is before me in its entirety. It is something I can see. I can avoid it, go around it, remove it. A mystery, however, surrounds and encompasses me. Instead of something to avoid or remove, it is something "in which I find myself caught up, and whose essence is therefore not to be before me in its entirety. It is as though in this province the distinction between *in me* and *before me* loses its meaning."[22] Rudolf Otto approaches the same reality in his classic *Idea of the Holy* by speaking of mystery as *tremendum*, as that before which the natural, human, and appropriate response is awe; and *fascinans*, that which provokes, fascinates, lures, and draws us in.[23] In some religious traditions, two further qualifications of mystery appear. In the first qualification, that which has always been understood as the fundamental mystery is God, the Incomprehensible Other (for example, as found in Karl Rahner's theology) who can never be named; and who, when felt as possessed, has been by that very feeling lost. However, because of the Jewish and Christian doctrine of the *Imago Dei*, which teaches that human beings are created in the image of this Incomprehensible Other, the notion of mystery spills over into human life as well. Made in the image of divinity, we, too, are mysteries.

A second meaning or qualification, which is more central to

Christian tradition and dominant in Catholicism and Ortho-doxy, comes from the Latin word *sacramentum*, which is a trans-lation of the Greek word *musterion*. Although both words have secular meanings, the meaning that has become embedded in Christianity is of a hidden, unseen, profound presence that becomes visible and tangible in persons, in events, and in things. This is the "persistently central assumption that certain objects or actions or words or places belonging to the ordinary spheres of life may convey to us a unique illumination of the whole mystery of our existence, because in these actions and reali-ties . . . something numinous is resident, something holy and gracious."[24] The most revered symbol of this persistent assump-tion, which Nathan Scott calls the "sacramental imagination," is the Christian Eucharist.

THE NUMINOUS

The foregoing description of mystery contains the word "nu-minous." Here we find a second qualifier of the religious on which I will draw in this book. The numinous refers to the experience we human beings know when we find ourselves ex-periencing an awareness of the presence of "divinity." What we *call* the divinity differs throughout the world, and even within particular communions; but the awareness is universal and often characterized as being in the sphere of holiness, awe, wonder. Ineluctably, and often without any warning, we find ourselves in the presence of a "Thou."[25] Something or someone cloaks us with its presence, and no amount of reasoning, evidence, or argument is able to dissuade us of this presence. In very simple language, the numinous is the "more than," the super-abundance of being we may suddenly confront in both the homeliest and the most exquisitely ineffable moments of our lives. It can touch us during the baby's bath, while eating a meal, on a dance floor, on a basketball court, during a peace demonstration, while making love, while typing a letter, or while washing the dishes. For most of us, it is a fleeting kind of presence:

> . . . only the unattended
> Moment, the moment in and out of time,

The distraction fit, lost in a flash of sunlight
The wild thyme unseen, or the winter lightning
Or the waterfall, or music heard so deeply
That it is not heard at all, but you are the music
While the music lasts[26]
　　　　　—T. S. Eliot "The Dry Salvages"

Nevertheless, and although fleeting, the numinous has the quality of permanence; once known it cannot be unknown.

THE MYSTICAL

A third quality of the religious that I wish to highlight is the mystical—the sense, belief, and awareness that at some fundamental level, everyone and everything is related to everyone and everything else. It is not possible to define the mystical with any precision. Indeed, Harvey Egan, one of our foremost scholars writing on mysticism today, suggests there may be as many as several hundred, often irreconcilable, definitions.[27] Nonetheless, in speaking of the essential connectedness of everyone and everything, I hope I am not doing violence to the core of mysticism but rather am appealing to that human sense of connectedness that has taken a variety of forms: the cosmic consciousness, where the entire universe can reveal the divine; *satori,* human spirit's pancosmic unity with all things at the moment of death; the Native American's communion with land and sky and animal; Wordsworth's nature mysticism, where knowing the essence of one flower in a crannied wall makes the knowing of everything else possible. Thus, when Walter Stace defines mysticism as "the apprehension of an ultimate nonsensuous unity in all things, a oneness or a One to which neither the senses nor reason can penetrate,"[28] he does, by centering on unity and oneness, say something about the nature of mysticism that is quite true. Since my purpose is to highlight essential qualities of the religious, I include the mystical to round out religious understanding, to lead to and to illuminate the final point I wish to make.

The point is this: I am convinced that to use such words as *mystery, the numinous,* and *mysticism*—in whatever context—is to speak a particular kind of language, a religious language, a language that draws on the symbols and images of religious traditions. The words have a resonance in flesh and psyche born from centuries of human attempt to speak the divine, to say the Unsayable, to name the Unnameable. Set in the midst of ordinary discourse, they are attempts to address the nonordinary. They are, if you will, specialized ways of using language. Nevertheless, they possess their own inner logic and inner meaning. Certainly it is appropriate to choose to use such language; its use is also distinguishable from other choices. I strain at this point since it is crucial for any further discourse about imagination if that word is to be preceded by the term *religious*.

Further, to speak about bringing the religious imagination to bear on the act of teaching is to assume some common universe of discourse, an assumption that cannot be made unless some common understandings are presented and—at least for the sake of argument—entertained. Once they are, as I have tried to do above, certain further suggestions can be offered. First, I propose that religion provides a way to speak about, qualify, distinguish, deepen, and direct imagination. When brought to bear upon teaching, the religious imagination enables us to see teaching through another lens. It enables us to pose the possibility that to dwell as a teacher with other human beings is to dwell in the area of *mystery*, not because subject matter is dense, but because we humans as the *Imago Dei* are ourselves mysteries, and interaction between us always takes place on holy ground, the only kind of ground there is.[29] To be teachers of any subject matter, whether physics or chemistry or marketing or sports, is to place ourselves in a setting where the *numinous* might appear, for anything and everything is capable of being flooded with the presence of divinity. And to believe in the *mystical* element of human life points paradoxically to the social and political dimensions in the act of teaching, since the belief that all things are related makes every word said in the activity of teaching— and about the activity of teaching—a word that, by extension, may be said about everything and everyone else in the universe.

IMAGINATION AS RELIGIOUS IMAGINATION

Having begun a tentative and as yet incomplete exploration of some of the meanings both of imagination and of the religious, I come now to the final task of this chapter. I want to examine the ways imagination appears to operate, by drawing on the seminal and immensely fruitful work of Philip Wheelwright in *The Burning Fountain*.[30] However, I also wish to reinterpret Wheelwright's "ways" by suggesting the religious dimensions of each. In doing so, I hope to illuminate and illustrate an initial meeting of the religious, the imagination, and that particular form of the gift I call the religious imagination.

Instead of exploring imagination from a psychological perspective, Wheelwright's starting point—and my own—is the poetic or artistic imagination. He regards four main emphases as central to imagination, and he points out that their interrelations supply much of the creative force that goes into the making of poetry. As ways of valuing are complementary, so, too, are these ways. The first is the *confrontative imagination*, which acts by particularizing, and seeing the other in its radical and unrepeatable uniqueness. It is the nature of the confrontative imagination *not to* generalize; to see what it is looking at as a Thou; to be present, to be immediate, to be there. When the confrontative imagination is at work, it is not immediately seeking to synthesize and to fuse disparate elements. Instead, it seeks to intensify its object. Thus, when this "way" of imagination is brought to bear on teaching, it looks at the activity in such a way that the confrontative imagination itself assumes a unique and often beautiful essence as part of teaching. Speaking of the concreteness of confrontative imagination, Wheelwright says that poetry is love and only the concrete is loved.[31] Later, I will explore the possibility that teaching may also be an adequate object of human love, and that at its best teaching is a way of being that possesses "ontological tenderness."[32]

The second form or way imagination operates is as the *distancing imagination*. When we operate by way of the distancing imagination, in contrast to the confrontative, we exercise restraint, discipline, and a certain tentativeness toward that which is before us. A seminal essay of Edward Bullough on psychical distance conveys the flavor of this form of imagining; he speaks of the kind of distancing where we put the phenomenon being observed out of gear with our practical, actual self; this disengagement then allows us to see the phenomenon with a freshness and a certain objectivity.[33] The problem caused by this way of imagining is too much objectivity; by putting us so far away from our practical, actual self, an *over*distancing often occurs, and the circuit of imaginative activity is broken. Yet the distancing imagination is needed to give room for its object to be itself, and here the key for the artist has always been the capacity to stylize. By working through the medium of style, the artist avoids intrusion and preserves necessary discipline.

The third way or form of imagination is often the only one addressed in reflection on the issue, or it is assumed to be synonymous with imaginative activity in its totality. This is the *compositive imagination,* whose essence is the blending of disparate elements. Wheelwright contends that two complementary metaphysical principles are necessary for this form of imagination. The first is *radical interpenetration;* the second is *radical novelty.* The first is related to the notion of mysticism articulated above: namely, in everything that exists there is a bit of everything else. This principle allows for the making of—or the discovery of—connections characteristic of all genuine composition that can accurately be called imaginative. The second principle, equally necessary, allows for the freshness and novelty by which we identify the genuinely creative, the "original." It is the power to put together, to harmonize elements that have never been brought together in exactly this way before. We see these principles incarnated in artists such as Van Gogh, Mozart, and Emily Dickinson. Peasants' boots have existed for centuries, but Van Gogh's paintings allow us to see them continually afresh. Mozart's "Haffner Serenade" creates melody as it has never been heard, even though the tones are the ordinary stuff of music. Emily Dickinson used simple words, "I never saw a moor . . . and yet I know what heather's like . . . " to give all of us—no matter where we live—the smell and feel and sight of Scotland. Whenever we use the compositive form of imagination, we, too, are engaged in the experience of interpenetration and novelty coming together. Indeed this form of imagination is the one that leads us to discover meaning, since all meaning, writes Wheelwright,

> . . . has as its subjective condition a certain mental responsiveness—a readiness to make connections and to associate this with that, a readiness

to see this and that in a single perspective, as forming a single individ-
uality, a single semantic object, an *ousia,* a Something Meant.[34]

Finally, there is a fourth way of imagination, the *archetypal
imagination.* This is the capacity to see the particular as embodying in some way a more universal significance, perhaps a
higher or deeper meaning than it carries in itself alone. The
word "archetype" is, of course, closely associated with Jungian
psychology, but it is the philosophical dimension I wish to note
here: whatever is seen, although it remains itself, can also be
an eminent instance of something else—for example, mythical
figures and personalities from literature can represent us to
ourselves. The special character of archetypal imagining is,
nonetheless, neither to exemplify nor even less to stand as allegory. Rather, this way of imagination, by the manner in which
it addresses the particular object, reveals in an almost effortless
way the universe or universal embedded within it. Let me offer
a pertinent example: I believe it is possible to see teaching as
an archetype, as an eminent instance for the other activities of
human vocation. What can be posited of teaching as imaginative
activity may also be true of companion activities such as coun-
seling, therapy, social advocacy, and administration, and of other
human professions farther afield: law, medicine, politics, home-
making, engineering.

RELIGIOUS IMAGINATION: A NEW INTERPRETATION

Drawing on Wheelwright's work, I now come to an underlying
assumption of this book. Another language for naming the ways
of imagination is available to us: religious language. I believe
the choice of religious language is an act of disclosure or revelation that enables us to "see" the religious quality of imagination, the deep and profound dimensions lying beneath its surface.
If the function of language is to give form to our experience of
the world, then the use of religious language to speak of imagination can help us understand the mysterious, the numinous,
and the mystical elements residing at the heart of the world,
including the world of teaching. My own conviction is that when
imagination is explored from the perspective of the religious,

and when that exploration addresses teaching, the holiness within teaching itself is more readily claimed and reclaimed, more readily released. I am also convinced that religious language is not arbitrary, and that Paulo Freire is correct in saying that semantics matter, words matter. An operating force pulses in words themselves, which can either obscure or reveal.[35]

This, to my mind, is a central and critical point. And what is the point, especially for teachers, teachers of religion, teachers of theology, teachers of teachers? Just this: Our thinking and our knowing in all human endeavor is shaped by the metaphors we employ. It *matters* which words we choose when we teach and when we teach others to teach. The metaphors we choose can catalyze or paralyze the capacity to perceive and receive what is there, no matter how plain or abundant the evidence. It is not that any of us willfully refuse to look; it is that if we do not have the appropriate language, we cannot see. And the reason the point is crucial is that words not only can paralyze, they can redeem.[36] Paul Ricoeur assures us that people are not motivated by direct appeals to the will. People are moved by experiencing their imaginations touched by someone or something that excites them into hoping and acting. When the word is made flesh, redemption is at hand. It is the vocation of the teacher to give flesh to language and to make metaphor incarnate.

Thus, when I come to speak of the religious imagination and teaching, I can continue to use the terms confrontative, distancing, compositive, and archetypal; or, following the teacher's vocation mentioned above, I can turn to the terms *contemplative, ascetic, creative,* and *sacramental.* These draw on the original terms without doing them violence. But they also expand and broaden and change those original terms, and give a new meaning to imagination. They give it a religious meaning. I do not choose these new terms arbitrarily, but out of the religious— and, in my own case, the religiously Christian—tradition that has actually helped shape them. Thus, I and others are able to draw not only on the terms or words themselves, but also—and importantly—on the vital operating power and connotations the religious tradition gives to these words as they resonate in the flesh and blood of the people who have made up the tradition through the centuries.

This renaming, in turn, leads to a discovery of the religious character of the imagination. The notion of the imagination as *contemplative* not only preserves the radical particularity and intensifying of Wheelwright's first form (the confrontative), the confronting of the other as a Thou, but it also enriches and deepens it by bringing all the associations of the religious activity of contemplation to bear as well. It incorporates the active intensity of the contemplative life, which calls for a totally engaged bodily presence: attending, listening, being-with, and existing fully in the presence of Being. It incorporates the cleanness of mind and clarity of sight which enables awareness of the other. It is a reminder of the mystical possibilities which reside within us all.

Similarly to reinterpret and then broaden the *distancing imagination* to become the *ascetic imagination* is to bring to bear all the understandings associated with religious discipline and discipleship. These include the need for detachment in the presence of the other, the letting be of being, the standing back in order not to violate. The way of the ascetic imagination is especially important to the activity of teaching. The power inherent in the teaching activity can often be used manipulatively and coercively, not only with reference to people, but with reference to the subject matter in the disciplines of study as well. Working with an ascetic imagination, however, the teacher is not only able to exercise respect and restraint toward both students and subject matter, the teacher is also able to avoid the danger of being too distanced, too removed from daily life. The ascetic imagination helps the teacher teach sympathetically and empathetically, but always with the reverence and respect other people demand and need. The ascetic imagination can act as the guarantor of the sacred in every human being.

Third, reinterpreting the compositive imagination as the *creative imagination* brings to bear an entire theology of creation embedded in religious tradition. Drawing on creative imagination, the teacher at work with learners can more easily see her or his work as creating new possibilities on every teaching occasion, as continually offering to others the opportunity to take the material presented and to reform and recreate it in and through themselves. Such activity can lead to the conclusion that as long as creation is at the center of teaching, what seem like final solutions are merely tentative—the status quo can always be changed. For those who believe that human beings are made in the image of a Creator God, this use of imagination can tap the potential of all to be creators. It can lead to the use of their potential in the service of one another and of the world.

Finally, if we allow sacrament the meaning of mystery as well as the power to reveal the presence of the holy, the gracious, the divine, Wheelwright's archetypal imagination can be religiously rendered as the *sacramental imagination.* Teaching seen through the lens of the *sacramental imagination* becomes not only Eminent Instance for other activities, but teaching itself becomes a sacrament, a symbolic, ritual form through which the holy is mediated. At the same time, teaching as a sacramental activity can also point out that all of life—all of human work—is capable of being sacrament. The Teilhardian insight applies here: For those who know how to see—really to *see*—nothing here on earth is profane. The next chapter examines the teaching activity in depth; as contemplative, as ascetic, as creative, and as sacramental. We will explore teaching as a work of religious imagination.

2. Teaching

Several years ago, while teaching a course called "Religious Models of Teaching," I asked the students to answer the question, "What is teaching?" in Haiku form. Bill Maroon wrote:

> We meet awkwardly.
> I invite you to walk.
> I find you dancing.

Bill's poem captures some of the beauty, artistry, and depth of the teaching activity. For me, the poem continues to be one of the richest understandings of the teaching act I have ever been taught. More than that, it provides an example of a way of talking about, or of approaching teaching that is all too rare: the way of imagination.

The rarity of this approach to teaching can be illustrated from a number of perspectives. One might look, for example, at teaching as it is presented in introductory manuals for beginning teachers, whether these are manuals used in schools of education dealing with teacher training or in volunteer situations such as church schools. In such manuals we find a heavy emphasis on assessing the needs of students, setting goals and objectives, designing learning activities to meet these goals and objectives, and evaluation. Such presentations appear to assume that teaching is just a technical skill and that one can learn it much as one learns how to ride a bicycle. With new teachers, especially if they are preparing to teach children, introduction to teaching too often comes in methods courses where the bulk of attention is given to techniques, procedures, and exercises. Although this approach is not entirely unnecessary, it can forestall a broader, deeper understanding of the teaching act.[1]

In direct contrast to the above, other approaches to teaching assume that one can automatically teach without giving much thought at all to what teaching means. This assumption is often present in college and graduate school teaching, where possession of a Ph.D. indicates "mastery" of subject matter in any area from physics to philosophy and apparently presupposes "mastery" of the matter of teaching as well. Supposedly, if one "knows" a particular area of study (a particular discipline), one also knows how to teach that discipline. I suspect that generations of school-age children have been turned away from the romance of learning by the pervasive understanding of teaching as equivalent with the first approach. I also suspect that generations of graduate students and older adults have been thoroughly bored and kept from entering new worlds by the prevalence of the second.

These two understandings of teaching are not very different; in fact, they share the same basic view: Teaching is a matter of content and method. The first understanding emphasizes method; the second emphasizes content. The question that needs to be asked about both emphases, however, is whether either method or content are the most appropriate ways to think about teaching in the first place. I will attempt to respond to that question and thus to overcome some of the limitations of the two perspectives. (I do not want to be read as entirely rejecting the first attitude, which, I believe, does have some place in an overall vision of teaching. On the other hand, neither do I want to reject the testimony experience offers concerning the existence of natural teaching genius—the presence in our midst of the "born teacher." Further, I do not wish to ignore the enormous contributions already being made by such teachers of teachers as Sara Little of Richmond, Dwayne Huebner of Yale, and Elliot Eisner of Stanford, as well as the contributions being made to further the study of teaching at such institutions as the Center for the Study of Teaching at the University of Michigan. Certainly I am not the first to decry the trivialization of the teaching act.)

I offer, however, an alternative vision of teaching, a vision that draws on the *religious imagination*. I am convinced that our society desperately needs a philosophy of teaching that explores the dimension of depth in teaching, a philosophy that begins not with technique but with the majesty and the mystery involved in teaching. To return to Marcel's distinction, I want to move away from teaching seen as a problem, to a view that assumes it is far more appropriate to see teaching as a mystery. With William Walsh, I believe that "all too many of the problems of education are mysteries made shabby by the absence of reverence."[2]

Because imagination is the root of the following description of teaching, it must be approached with fresh eyes. Rather than address teaching as a technical skill, then, I suggest we bring to it an attitude similar to that which we bring to any work of art. Such an attitude implies a beginning readiness to see what is there and to let what is there speak, rather than an immediately active attitude that sees teachers as agents, doers, and performers. The imaginative attitude implies, initially, an attitude of receptivity.

This process has emerged over the last two decades in my own work with both beginning and experienced teachers. We have discovered in our work together that teaching is analogous to any work of creation. That discovery was initially made in working with clay: We felt the clay, pummeled it, played with it, found out what it could do and not do; what we could do to it and with it and in interchange with it. In this book work with clay will be a basic metaphor to facilitate an understanding of how teaching may be a work of religious imagination.

The process has five moments, or steps: (1) contemplation, (2) engagement, (3) formgiving, (4) emergence, and (5) release. The steps envisioned, however, are not like steps on a staircase, progressing upwards. Rather, they are like steps in a dance, where movement is both backward and forward, around and through, and where turns, returns, rhythm, and movement are essential.[3] Indeed, it will probably be apparent that each step is present in all of the others.

A PARADIGM FOR TEACHING

The process is also offered as a paradigm. *Mutatis mutandis* (the necessary changes being made), it has a universality that makes it symbolic of other human actions. It calls for a certain rigor. And its pattern is organic in the sense that each step flows out of the one preceding it. From this, it should be clear that

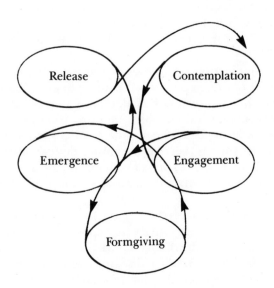

each one of the steps, in its own way, draws on the four forms of imagination outlined in chapter 1 as the ways, forms, or paths of religious imagination. The reflection or attitude of receptivity demanded in the exploration is a work of contemplation; the rigor is an act of asceticism; the bringing together of disparate elements is an act of creation; and the universality claimed is an argument for the sacramental quality of the process.

CONTEMPLATION

The first moment in teaching seen as a work of religious imagination is contemplation.[4] The task is to begin the teaching activity by seeing what is there. Thus we do not begin by preparing our material, we begin by being still. In this moment, we are asked to see teaching as a Thou, so that we might bring to it an attitude of silence, reverence, and respect.

In traditional religious usage, the term *contemplation* implies a totally uncluttered appreciation of existence, a state of mind or a condition of the soul that is simultaneously wide-awake and free from all preoccupation, preconception, and interpretation.[5]

In a remarkable passage from *Pilgrim at Tinker Creek,* Annie Dillard conveys something of what is involved in this moment. The passage is worth recording in its entirety.

When I was six or seven years old, growing up in Pittsburgh, I used to take a precious penny of my own and hide it for someone else to find. It was a curious compulsion; sadly, I've never been seized by it since. For some reason I always "hid" the penny along the same stretch of sidewalk up the street. I would cradle it at the roots of a sycamore, say, or in a hole left by a chipped-off piece of sidewalk. Then I would take a piece of chalk, and, starting at either end of the block, draw huge arrows leading up to the penny from both directions. After I learned to write, I labeled the arrows: SURPRISE AHEAD or MONEY THIS WAY. I was greatly excited, during all this arrow-drawing, at the thought of the first lucky passerby who would receive in this way, regardless of merit, a free gift from the universe. But I never lurked about, I would go straight home and not give the matter another thought, until, some months later, I would be gripped again by the impulse to hide another penny.

It is still the first week in January, and I've got great plans. I've been thinking about seeing. There are lots of things to see, unwrapped gifts and free surprises. The world is fairly studded and strewn with pennies cast broadside from a generous hand. But—and this is the point— who gets excited by a mere penny? If you follow one arrow, if you crouch motionless on a bank to watch a tremulous ripple thrill on the water and are rewarded by the sight of a muskrat kit paddling from its den, will you count that sight a chip of copper only, and go your rueful way? It is dire poverty indeed when a man is so malnourished and fatigued that he won't stoop to pick up a penny. But if you cultivate a healthy poverty and simplicity, so that finding a penny will literally make your day, then, since the world is in fact planted in pennies, you have with your poverty bought a lifetime of days. It is that simple. What you see is what you get.[6]

What you see is what you get. In some ways, this is the essence of contemplation; cultivating the healthy virtues of poverty and simplicity which make us ready for the seeing, and then discovering that the seeing is a necessary condition for hope, for possibility, for the future. If we return to the notion that we begin the act of teaching with such seeing (with contemplation) what do we discover?

I submit that we first discover the human coming together

essential at the core of teaching. The teacher finds herself or himself in the presence of, and called to be at the disposal of, other human beings who have come into the teacher's presence ready to learn, to know, to be instructed.[7] Such a circumstance is perhaps most obvious with first-graders on the first day of school—eyes shining, pencils sharpened, trust still flowing from their bodies as they put themselves in the teacher's care. But it is also a circumstance with adults. During my own long years in graduate school, I have yet to encounter someone who on the first day of a course in any semester will not respond when asked, "How did it go?" with an answer on the order of, "I think it is going to be good." For me, that answer symbolizes the contemplative moment where the readiness (for teaching and learning) involves the student's seeing the teacher as a Thou; the hope that the teacher, before seeing the student as student, will also see a Thou; and the additional hope that a community of partners learning and studying together will be created. Thus, the first object of contemplation is seeing teaching as a work where a community of people come together as a community of hope; a coming together of people, each of whom brings her or his radical particularity as *this* unique person. The first moment in teaching (contemplation) is the stopping, the taking time, the wide-awakeness necessary to "take in" the personhood(s) involved. What you see is what you get.

In teaching, however, there are not only two elements, the teacher and the student; in teaching there is always a third element, the subject matter. The two people do not come together to address one another, they come together in the presence of a third, which, in May Sarton's phrase, "fuses us at moments into a whole."[8] The presence of this third element allows for the psychical distance necessary for learning. Like all stereotypes, the stereotype of group discussion, crass as it often seems, bears some truth, and can serve to illustrate the absolute necessity of the third element's presence in teaching. Usually expressed as, "And what shall we talk about today?" the stereotype captures the emptiness created when the third partner, subject matter, is not present; without the third partner a necessary condition for teaching collapses. The added dimension contemplation brings to teaching is not *that* this third element exists. Rather contemplation helps us realize that subject matter is also a Thou, a third partner, if you will. Just as learners must be themselves, with all of their hopes and dreams, their capacities and unfaith, so that which is being addressed together in the teaching act must also be *itself*.

This realization gives several clues to the teacher about the teaching situation. It directs the teacher (the first partner) to see the thing being presented as itself, and to move with care when interpreting, analyzing, and explaining. At the same time, it also gives space to the learners (the second partner) and allows them to become familiar with the subject matter (the third partner), so that they, too, might engage in initial contemplation. At the beginning (and one way of thinking of every teaching event is to see it as the capacity for beginning), we seek the primary receptive moment where ordinary knowing slows for a moment, and not-knowing enters, silently enabling encounter to occur. A too-quick move to cover the material can end in covering over the material.

The act of teaching itself, the people involved, and the subject matter: These are the first three objects of contemplation. But one more needs mentioning. The act of teaching demands a contemplation of the environment, that is, of the context or the situation in which the teaching takes place. This refers not only to the physical setting and to such mundane elements as chairs, desks, carpets, temperature, and time, but to the social, political, and economic environment as well. A tactic that experienced teachers incorporate to ensure this aspect of contemplation is previsualization, imagining and seeing in the mind's eye the place that will be entered and the people who will be entering that place together. This element in teaching is what Elliot Eisner calls the "implicit curriculum."[9] My concern here is simply to name it as a factor in the teaching act. It is an essential partner in the teaching activity, acting upon, acting with, and sometimes acting against it. In other words, the environment, too, deserves awareness, silence, attention, and respect.

ENGAGEMENT

The second moment in the teaching process is best named engagement. Having fulfilled the requirement to stand back and to be still, the teacher must now gather the disparate ingredients (or elements) in teaching and catalyze them toward re-creation. Engagement means diving in, wrestling with, and rolling around in subject matter. Engagement brings the contemplative imagination to bear on something tangible, and makes the creative (compositive) imagination active. Just as sculptors move from feeling, touching, testing, learning about, and contemplating clay, to the moment of getting their hands and fingers involved in it (engaging it), teachers must also move beyond gazing at and apprising to the far more active work of interaction, interchange, and "messing with" the subject matter.

In teaching, as in any work of art, however, the moment of engagement may be resisted. Artist Ben Shahn suggests that three obstacles keep us from genuine engagement. The first obstacle is dilettantism, the nonserious dabbling in what is presumably a very serious matter. The second is fear of our own creativity. And the third is the misconception of what kind of a person an artist is.[10] Each of these obstacles must be overcome in order to be genuinely engaged.

To become genuinely engaged, we must first take seriously the nature and the meaning of subject matter. Otherwise, dilettantism is almost inevitable. For the teacher, the engagement must begin through involvement with subject matter at the deepest and most profound level: Subject matter must be loved. Although this is not always possible to explain, it is possible to exemplify. This poem by James Worley describes a teacher as an engaged lover.

Mark Van Doren (1946)

You know, he didn't teach me any *thing*;
The Chaucer, Edmund Spenser, Dante—wait!
I'm often etched by what he said of trimmers
(or by what he said that Dante said of them)
that they weren't wanted, even down in hell—
but otherwise (and that's the wise he was)
he taught me not a thing that I've remembered.

Why, then, is he the uppermost in mind
when I am asked—most often by myself—
"Who was the finest teacher you have known?"

The style, the style's the trick that keeps him kept—
no, not a trick; it must unfold as grace,
inevitably, necessarily,
as tomcats stretch, as sparrows scrounge for lice:
in such a way he lolled upon his desk
and fell in love before our very eyes
again, again—how many times again!—
with Dante, Chaucer, Shakespeare, Milton's Satan,
as if his shameless, glad, compelling love
were all he really wanted us to learn;
no, that's not right; we were occasionals
who lucked or stumbled or were pushed on him—
he fell in love because he fell in love;
we were but windfall parties to those falls.[11]

What is needed to understand subject matter in such a way? I suggest it is the realization, initially, that the term "subject matter," hides an equivocation. To quote William Walsh,

It is often assumed that there is some necessary relation between the educated mind and a wide range of scholarship, a notion to which university teachers are especially prone. But this seems to be a dubious assumption. It is founded on the habit of thinking of subject matter in a grossly materialistic way as an area to be covered, or as a volume to be exhausted or a bulk to be chipped at. It is confirmed by the other habit of taking subject matter as a single instead of a double concept. But the term subject-matter disguises an equivocation. It conflates two related but distinct meanings. On the one hand any subject-matter is a system of clues, concerned with human existence, organized about some initiating and defining concept, expressed in language and argued by human beings. On the other hand, subject matter is that world of meaning, order of nature, physical process, pattern of events, organization of feelings which the former kind of subject matter enables us to conceive. It is that labyrinth of reality through which and towards the understanding of which any particular discourse is a directing and guiding thread.[12]

Walsh concludes by asserting that unless subject matter in the first sense empowers us to understand subject matter in the second sense, it fails to serve its purpose. Unfortunately, this is precisely what all too much contemporary teaching does. My own suspicion is that such failure is inevitable if the meaning of the act of teaching is understood only as a set of procedures or methods designed to present subject matter; and if subject matter is assumed to *be* that system of clues concerned with human existence, organized about some initiating and defining concept, *and nothing more.*

However, if subject matter is appreciated and seen as the world of meaning, order of nature, physical process, pattern of events, "labyrinth of reality" toward which the system of clues has been designed to point, then a richness of meaning to subject matter appears. This richness helps lessen the fear of our own creativity (the second obstacle to engagement mentioned above), for it allows the subject matter its own character, inviolability, and power to address. Our own creativity as teachers is not the only creativity operating, however. A creative dynamic exists in the subject matter as well. Put another way, neither teacher nor student(s) needs to "do it all." Subject matter is also a partner in the learning process. Engaged playing with the meaning of subject matter leads to further discovery. Beginning with Walsh's insights into the term "subject matter" as having *two* senses or meanings—first, the system of clues, second, subject matter as labyrinth of reality—I would suggest a third and a fourth.

The third meaning of subject matter is beyond, under, over, and essentially related to the first two: Human beings are subjects, even more, subjects who matter in the sense Paulo Freire has taught us.

For Freire, authentic human existence pivots precisely on this point. In his brilliant and truly creative educational philosophy, authentic existence demands freedom, and the conflict preceding and leading to that freedom is one between either being a spectator to one's own reality or being an actor who initiates her or his own activity toward the world, an actor who is *engaged.* For human beings, the essential decision is between speaking or remaining embedded in a culture of silence, between naming oneself or being named by others, between remaining an object or *becoming a subject.* Here is the heart of Freire's vision: What makes human beings human is that each of us has an *ontological vocation to be a subject,* namely, one who can separate from the world in his or her own consciousness, be critical of it, act on it, and transform it—in the process making the world a subject, too.[13]

Before looking at the fourth meaning of subject matter, we must now return to Shahn's third obstacle, the misunderstanding of what it is to be an artist. We misunderstand what it is to be a teacher if we think that teaching simply means to hand on, hand over, or convey subject matter merely as a system of clues. Actually, teaching is far more. Teaching is the creation of a situation in which subjects, human subjects, are handed over to *themselves*. Thus, when we understand that engagement with subject matter means engagement with human beings as subjects, we can also see how the contemplative moment is incorporated into the moment of engagement, where our ontological vocation to be subjects not only requires us to be engaged with the world, but also to stand back and to look at how we look at the world. As engaged subjects, engaging with subject matter, we are contemplative subjects as well.

Based on the above, we can now look at a fourth and final sense or meaning of "subject matter," one which is consonant with Jewish and Christian tradition: namely, the belief in a Creator divinity, always acting in human affairs, holding all in being by its sacred presence. Theological doctrine would describe this belief by using a phrase such as "the Being of being." But for our discussion it seems more appropriate to speak of the Subjectivity of subjectivity: The belief that everything and everyone in existence draws that existence from participation in the One Who Is, and that any human subjectivity which exists does so by reason of its own being in, dwelling in, and having been created in the fullness, richness, and depth of the Subjectivity of God.[14]

Whenever I reread Martin Buber's classic essay on education, it is this last rendering of subject that captures my attention. Buber speaks of the educator discovering an inner religious impulse to be in the service of the One who is able to do what human beings cannot do: to create and form and transform. The educator is set in the *imitatio Dei absconditi sed non ignoti*: the imitation of the divinity who, although hidden from sight, is not unknown.[15] Once more we are met by the holiness of teaching. From the attitude of contemplation, we discover that the teacher is—through engagement with subject matter in all its renderings—someone called by, called with, and calling upon the Creator God to save, to perfect, and to manifest the divine image that dwells by reason of subjectivity in all existing being.

FORM-GIVING

One of the greatest teachers I have ever known was Mary Tully, my mentor at Union Seminary. She once gave us a simple exercise connected with clay. We first played with clay and discovered something of what it could do (for example, it could only be stretched so long, then it would break; too much air would harden it). Then we were asked to blindfold ourselves and to continue to work with the material. We had contemplated, we had become engaged, but now was the moment for us to interact with the clay and to give it form. As we dutifully blindfolded ourselves, Tully gave us the following directions: "A form exists within the ball of clay you are holding in your hands, and you are to find the form. But, you are to find it in the interchange with the clay; you are not to impose some prior vision of what is already there. So, take the time, concentrate, work with the clay and let it work with you, and in time you will discover that a form is taking shape. You will be able to feel it, to sense it, to intuit it. Once that happens, you can take off the blindfold and work from there."

I have often done that same exercise with others and discovered without a trace of doubt that Mary Tully was right. The form was there, is there, waiting to be found. The power of the clay metaphor is that it teaches us the nature of forming, informing, formation, and form-giving in the activity of teaching. It teaches us that teachers and students work together with material, contemplating it, engaging it, bringing to it as much as they possibly can; but that for true form-giving to occur, any and all prior absolute conviction regarding the exact nature of the form itself must be absent.

My own conviction is that form-giving is the paradoxical center of teaching. It is the moment when preparation, prior knowledge, and the understanding of subject matter as a system of clues is essential. At the same time, it is the moment when all the learning may produce something quite unexpected, the paradox being that the preknown, the finished, is needed. The teacher's presence at this moment is essential; the teacher acts very directly, but the quality of the teacher's involvement is, in Buber's phrase, through a "strange paradox." The teacher carefully selects and prepares from the actual world that which is to be presented. But, "if education means to let a selection of the world affect a person through the medium of another person, then the one through whom this takes place, rather who makes it take place through himself, is caught in a strange paradox."[16] Buber concludes that the paradox is that one must always do this selection, prepare it, and present it "from the other side, from over there, from the surface of that other spirit which is being acted upon—not of some conceptual, contrived spirit, but all the time the wholly concrete spirit of this individual and unique being who is living and confronting the educator, and who stands together with the [teacher] in the common situation of educating and being educated."[17]

Of all the moments in teaching, perhaps none is more dependent on the exercise of the imagination than is form-giving. Not only does the power of imagination make formgiving possible, teaching in a form-giving way is possible only if the teacher *imagines* that it is possible; if the teacher imagines that *this* is what teaching is. If the teacher believes that teaching means merely to hand over ideas, facts, and concepts to be memorized, teaching is certain to fail. For in the step of form-giving the human being is, in Wordsworth's phrase, tenacious of the forms which it receives. The point to be remembered, however, is that the forms human beings strive for, and feel for, through all the darkness and blindfolding, are not "finished" thoughts (the French *pensée pensée*), but thought and reality and meaning "in the making," in the giving, in the going-through, in the living (the French *pensée pensanté*). The *only* forms that can be given are "the perspectives from which we see, the dimensions by which we grasp, the frames that stabilize, the categories that define and sort our experience."[18] In other words, forms are not our ideas, our concepts, our learning. They are, instead, the grounds of those ideas, the roots of learning, and the foundations of our lives: love, identity, death, intention, destiny, courage, hope.

In teaching as an activity of religious imagination, the moment of form-giving is the one where our creative imagination gives shape to the content or subject matter; form-giving is the *way* we attempt to put subject matter together. New form comes into being because we take the risk of becoming artists, becoming creators, becoming teachers. From form-giving flows the fourth step or moment in the teaching process: emergence.

EMERGENCE

Perhaps no passage about a teacher and a student working together is better known—at least in the English-speaking world—than the following:

She brought me my hat and I knew I was going out into the warm sunshine. This thought, if a wordless sensation can be called a thought, made me hop and skip with pleasure. We walked down the path to the well house, attracted by the fragrance of the honey-suckle with which it was covered. Someone was drawing water and my teacher placed my hand under the spout. As the cool stream gushed over one hand she spelled into the other the word *water*, first slowly, then rapidly. I stood still, my whole attention fixed upon the motions of her fingers. Suddenly, I felt a misty consciousness as of something forgotten—a thrill of returning thought: and somehow the mystery of language was revealed to me. I knew then that w-a-t-e-r meant the wonderful cool something that was flowing over my hand. That living word awakened my soul, gave it light, hope, joy, set it free! There were barriers still, it is true, but barriers that could in time be swept away.[19]

In this passage Helen Keller describes the moment of emergence, that point in the process of teaching where something new is being born, and where the learner takes possession of the received form.

Emergence is marked by tentativeness, by a gathering of strength, and by a beginning possession, not by completeness and security. Because of this, emergence is often characterized by "I think I've got it," followed by "I lost it," followed by "I think I've got it," with repetitive frequency. (One thinks, for example, of Eliza Doolittle at the Ascot races forced to speak "proper English" too soon; she hasn't yet "got it." Eliza's true moment of emergence—let it not be forgotten that *My Fair Lady* is the story of a teacher and a student—comes with her unforgettable declaration, "The rain in Spain stays mainly in the plain." And then Henry Higgins can say, "She's got it; by George, she's got it.")

Most moments of emergence are not as dramatic as Helen Keller's or Eliza Doolittle's. Nonetheless, they all signal a movement of the teaching act toward its completion. They all say that although something new is beginning to be born, that something is connected to what has gone before; but for the present moment, in this learner, in this situation, subject matter is being and has been reformed, indeed reinvented for the future with a life of its own. Emergence may best be characterized as awesome, since although its coming can never be controlled or predicted, its happening is unmistakable, irrevocable, and not unlike birth. Emergence is the herald of new life.

The temporality and the rhythm in teaching is perhaps nowhere as evident as it is in emergence. What happens in the moment of emergence may be quite different from what was expected. "Perhaps the greatest of all pedagogical fallacies," said John Dewey, "is that people learn the thing they are studying at the time they are studying it."[20] More seriously, the moment of emergence has an inner requirement: It needs to occur in its own time, and not on a schedule constricted by semester or term, by examination or pressure. Perhaps the following passage from *Zorba the Greek* can help us to understand this better.

I remembered one morning when I discovered a cocoon in the bark of a tree, just as the butterfly was making a hole in its case and preparing to come out. I waited a while, but it was too long appearing and I was impatient. I bent over it and breathed on it to warm it. I warmed it as quickly as I could and the miracle began to happen before my eyes, faster than life. The case opened, the butterfly started slowly crawling out and I shall never forget my horror when I saw how its wings were folded back and crumpled; the wretched butterfly tried with its whole trembling body to unfold them. Bending over it, I tried to help it with my breath. In vain. It needed to be hatched out patiently and the unfolding of the wings should be a gradual process in the sun. Now it was too late. My breath had forced the butterfly to appear, all crumpled, before its time. It struggled desperately and a few seconds later, died in the palm of my hand.

That little body is, I do believe, the greatest weight I have on my conscience. For I realize today that it is a mortal sin to violate the great laws of nature. We should not hurry, we should not be impatient, but we should confidently obey the eternal rhythm.[21]

The poignancy of the passage is evident: Too much pressure, too soon, violates the law of nature, the law of teaching, the law of eternal rhythm. But the passage also gives courage, especially to those entrusted with the young. It is a good thing to know—better—to be convinced that you do not have to do it all in the fourth grade, or in the primary school, or in the infant's room, even if you *are* the fourth-grade teacher or the primary-school teacher or the infant-school teacher. Likewise, you do not have to say the final word on sin even if you are the ethics professor. You do not have to speak the final word on living even if you are the mother, the father, the grandparent. Emergence happens silently, and one does violence to keep pulling up the plant to see if the roots are growing; emergence happens in divine time (in *illo tempore*) and not in ours. Emergence cannot be guaranteed. Indeed, emergence is a reminder to any teacher that for new life to be born, the teacher will probably have to live through periods of sadness and grieving and staying in the darkness, even to live through periods of mourning and of death. But if the teacher does so, a final moment in the teaching process is bound to occur.

RELEASE

We look again to working with clay to find an image of the final step of the teaching process. When we form new life out of clay (when we take off our blindfolds and see life occurring before our eyes), a great temptation confronts us. We find ourselves tempted to keep on working, to make one more line, to add one more design, to deepen just one hollow. When this happens, it is important for us to be aware that there is a point in the creative act of molding—as there is in the religious activity of teaching—where one must say, "I can do no more," and where the only right thing to do is to let go. This is the moment of release. Release acknowledges that one can do no more, that for whatever it is worth, new being is sent into the world, and the movement or moment or step now demanded of the teacher is cessation of movement, or rest, or emptiness.[22]

Swimming teachers sometimes begin teaching, especially if their charges are fearful, by keeping a strong and supportive hand under the stomach of the new swimmer. But all good teachers of swimming know that they must eventually remove their hand if any good is to happen. Release is the moment in teaching where we remove the hand, where we say to the other, "It is no longer mine; it is now yours." As with emergence, sadness can be, and often is, essential to the moment of release. In fact, release is a fine time to learn humility. The great teacher, to paraphrase Lao-Tzu, the people do not notice. The next they honor and praise. The next the people fear, and the last the people hate. When the great teacher's work is done, the people say, "Ah! We did it ourselves." In the moment of release, learning passes forever into the newly created vehicle, and the human response, the holy response, is not "the teacher did it," but, "Ah! We did it ourselves."

I argue for the *holiness* of the moment of release because of its echoes in the religious life of the world. Release is close to *satori,* the absence of desire and the fulfillment of desire at the same time. It is close to the Zen art of archery: In Zen the archer and arrow are one, here teacher and subject are one. It is also close to the *Hsing-Hsing Ming* of Zen, which says that when you strive to be quiet by stopping motion, the quiet you achieve is always in motion. It is akin to the full rest of Sabbath in Judaism, where the cessation of movement re-creates the world. It is the full emptiness of the *kenosis* known to Jesus of Nazareth, who emptied himself becoming obedient to death. Release is the moment of simplicity—Annie Dillard's healthy simplicity, true, but also the complete simplicity of T. S. Eliot "costing no less than everything."

But release, although the last moment, is not the culminating moment in the teaching process. Yes, release is the moment of rest, of emptiness, of stillness. But it is so only that out of release a new moment of contemplation may begin where the ascetic, creative, sacramental work starts once more.

And what necessity urges beginning again? Why continue? The answer to that question will be explored throughout the rest of this book. The simplest answer, however, is that the teaching process must continue because of the continuing demands of the situation; or, put more simply, because of the continuing demands of the world. In subsequent chapters, I will argue that teaching as an act of religious imagination is a power to re-create the world. For now, however, in focusing on the why behind this conviction, I can do no better than to recall the words of Nobel laureate Par Lagerkvist, whose poetic insight suggests a cosmic vocation.

> May my heart's disquiet never vanish;
> May I never be at peace;
> May I never be reconciled to life nor to death either;
> May my path be unending.[23]

Lagerkvist does not need to say more, but the teacher needs to be aware that the moment of release, with its Sabbath quietude, has a dynamism within it that allows us the possibility to hear the disquiet of the world. In the peace of release, the teacher is enabled to hear the agony of those human subjects who are not at peace. In the moment of reconciliation that release symbolizes, the teacher realizes she or he cannot be reconciled to life or death as they now occur on the planet, and that the teacher's path is unending because the world awaits re-creation.

Teachers, by reason of their vocation toward re-creation, must continue on this path. If they do, they discover the next station along the way. And since teaching is a vocation centered in the religious imagination, that station is incarnation. It is to the nature of incarnation in the teaching process that we shall turn in chapter 3.

3. Incarnation

The theme of this book has been with me for many years. I have always been intrigued by the notion that in the fields of religious education and religion teaching, psychology or science or sociology, rather than religion, provide the main categories of interpretation. To take what is perhaps the most obvious example, developmental theory has been more of a bible for religion teachers to understand their work than has been the biblical record itself. Thus, the idea of drawing on religion and imagining teaching as a *religious* activity has always struck me as work that needed to be done.

The *way* we speak about our teaching influences and determines what we *do* when we teach. For example, I can speak about teaching as the preparation of subject matter, the arranging of subject matter, or the organizing of subject matter, and I believe that teaching is all of that. But from a religious perspective, when I use the metaphor *incarnation* I begin to imagine the teaching activity differently and create the possibility that the metaphor itself influences the doing.

Therefore, I propose that teaching is the *incarnation* of subject matter. Incarnation is a word with much resonance in theology. Perhaps it resonates deepest in the Christian doctrine that states that in the person of Jesus of Nazareth, the Word of God became flesh. Even should a person not know of this doctrine, it has become so fixed in religious thought that it has at least a residual influence on the way we hear the term. (The *Oxford English Dictionary* refers to this doctrine, God taking flesh in the Christ, as "the earliest and still the most prevalent sense" of the term incarnation.) For example: In the Catholic liturgy, until the mid-1960s, when the Latin words *Et verbum caro factum est et habitavit in nobis*, "The Word was made flesh and dwelt among us," were recited at the conclusion of Mass during the "Last Gospel" (today, proclaimed as the Gospel for "Mass During the Day" on Christmas), the entire congregation *knelt* to give testimony to its belief in the world-changing character of the Incarnation event.

Along with this first meaning in religion—related of course to the literal meaning of *in-carne* as "in flesh"—other metaphorical understandings of incarnation have emerged. Thus, incarnation has come to be understood first as the putting into or assumption of a definite form, embodiment; and second as a person in whom some quality, attribute, or principle is exhibited in a bodily form—that is, a living type or representative or, again, an embodiment. I wish to draw on both of these meanings when speaking about teaching as the incarnation of subject matter. Teaching, understood as a work of religious imagination, is the incarnation, embodiment, giving-form-to, giving-flesh-to subject matter: to the ideas, concepts, and notions that are the system of clues; to the deeper meanings toward which those clues are directed; to the people who are participating subjects in existence, whose ontological vocation it is to be and to become subjects; and, perhaps, even to the Mystery whose identity as the Being of Being supports all of existence.

Another way of saying that teaching is the incarnation of subject matter is to say that teaching is the creation of form. The teacher is one who embodies—gives flesh to—form. But form is not an arbitrary organizational element. Every artist knows that form is not only the *intention* of content; it is the actual embodiment of content. Form is based on a theme. It is a marshaling of materials in relation to one another. It is a setting of boundaries and limits. It is a discipline, an ordering, and a shaping according to need.[1] Because of the variegated possibilities in subject matter, however, the teacher must learn not just one form, but a repertoire of forms in order to teach. If the teacher hopes to make subject matter available, or in the more illuminating term, "accessible,"[2] the teacher must bring to bear a variety of incarnational possibilities on and in the teaching act. On the one hand, this demand is urgent because human beings possess a wide range of ways of coming to know, to understand, and to learn. And on the other hand, that which people find themselves trying to learn—the ordinary "subject matter"—has its own inner demands to be formed, embodied, incarnated in ways that are true to *its* nature. Therefore, before moving to the major part of this chapter, which is a description and exemplification of the forms for subject matter, let me describe something of the range of the knowing subject, and then something of the inner demands of that which the knowing subject wants to learn.

THE KNOWING SUBJECT

The knowing subject possesses a broad range or variety of ways of learning: through concrete experience; through reflective observation; through abstract conceptualization; and through active experimentation. We call these "ways" different aspects of the learning act. And we can call the learning act a learning circle, as the following diagram illustrates[3]:

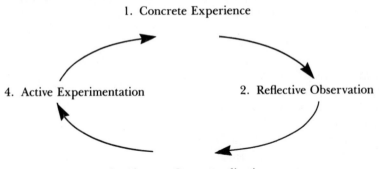

1. Concrete Experience

4. Active Experimentation

2. Reflective Observation

3. Abstract Conceptualization

Whenever, as a teacher, I find myself assisting others to learn, I am aware of the need to address all four ways of learning in the learning circle. The concrete experience may not necessarily be an activity where physical involvement of the entire body is involved, such as skating or swimming or dancing; it could be listening to a lecture, to the analysis or presentation of a body of ideas, or it could be taking part in a symposium. Yet, no matter what the particular concrete experience is, some initial referent, occurrence, and embodiment of subject matter always begins the process of learning. That embodiment is followed, at some point, with the opportunity for reflective observation, time to distinguish, to speculate, to be with, as an aid to clarification. Such reflection then moves one toward abstract conceptualization, toward creating some hypothesis or generalization to help solidify the concrete experience. The conceptualization, in turn, moves one to active experimentation.

Each of the four steps of the learning circle arises not only out of the step preceding it, but, in fact, out of all the steps preceding it. Thus, the fourth step of the learning circle, experimentation, is not the circle's culmination. Rather, just as the preceding steps led to the fourth, so does experimentation lead us to concrete experience, the first step, and the cycle begins again.

The above process happens naturally, indeed habitually, whenever we are in the act of learning. For example, I wake in the morning and gradually become aware that it is a Saturday, and I am free of obligations. That sets me to thinking about the possibilities I might choose. I consider each possibility according to some principle or judgment or hypothesis—"If I shop now, then . . . " or "If I go to the movies now, then . . . " or "If I want to visit the hospital, then . . . " After conceptualizing my possibilities, I decide on active experimentation.

Sometimes, of course, the process is very dramatic. I think of Louise Bruyn, Newton housewife, mother of three, opening the *Boston Globe* one day in the early 1970s. On opening the paper (concrete experience), she read the headline: "United States bombs neutral Cambodia." As Louise Bruyn tells the story, she remembers thinking about the headline, wondering what it might mean for her, what it demanded of her, what her being a Quaker might have to do with it (reflective observation). She formulated a principle: "I am opposed to this. If I act, if I do something, it might not change anything. But if I do nothing, no possibility for changing things exists at all" (abstract conceptualization). And so she did something, made a statement, decided to *walk* from Newton Center, Massachusetts, to Washington, D.C. as a way of saying, "No. As a citizen, I am saying No" (active experimentation).

Although this process is fairly universal, each of us will emphasize different aspects of it as we go about learning. For

example, some of us will be most comfortable in stressing concrete activity, giving ourselves time for encounter with, touching, probing, and "getting a sense" of the other through using
our senses. Others may want time enough to be watchers, wait-
ers, reflectors. We might be the silent ones, and our learning
will depend heavily on observation. Still others of us, who are
highly developed conceptually, will discover that our preferred
way of learning is to get at the concepts, the ideas, the general
principles. Finally, there are those of us whose characteristic
learning practice will be to try something, to be pragmatists,
learning best by coming to a decision about what works and
what does not work. Depending on who is learning what, we
will find that we start at different points on the learning circle.
Not all of us will begin with concrete experience; still, our
learning will be incomplete until we touch all four. From all of
this, two principles emerge: one for the learner, the other for
the thing to be learned.

First, none of us learns only through concrete experience;
each of us *needs* to learn through all four partners on the
learning circle. In fact, we are enriched in our knowing by the
more ways we can come at a subject matter; and we are poorer,
and straitened in our learning, when only one is used. Cultural
biases abound *for* one way over the other, but without doubt, the
culture that stresses only one way is the loser. Thus, the impli-
cation for a teacher seems to be to try to incarnate subject
matter in a variety of ways so that the full range of human
learning capacities may be developed in every learner.

At the same time, the second principle reminds us that because we do have our individual preferences for learning in
ways congenial to our particular dispositions or subcultures or
genes, we often find that we learn better in one mode than we
do in another. We may be visual or tactile or kinesthetic. We
may be slow or fast or middling. We may be dreamers or actors.
Think of the child of five, who is far more comfortable with the
concrete and the experimental; think of the nonliterate societies
of today and other centuries who value(d) sight and touch as
ways of knowing more than the verbalized word; think of the
contemplative visionary, most at home in the realms of search,
reflection, and quiet. Although each person has the capacity to
use many ways of learning, certain natural and historical biases

condition us toward one way more than toward another. Thus, all learners need to be encouraged in their natural modes, and not fitted arbitrarily into someone else's pattern.

INNER DEMANDS OF WHAT IS TO BE LEARNED

Just as the knowing subject needs a variety of ways of learning, so does the nature of subject matter demand a repertoire of forms. Some subjects are best embodied as concepts, others are not. The theory of relativity is a theory. Logical positivism is a philosophical concept. Chartres, in contrast, is a cathedral— a subject to be seen, to be experienced as a place of worship, and to be studied through touching the stone. Music is for hearing. Lectures are not the best way to understand the power of group process.

To complicate the matter, it needs also to be noted that like human beings as subjects, all other subjects benefit by being approached from a variety of perspectives. Thus, even though every subject (person or idea) will exhibit its own constraints, that is, make its own inner demands on the learner, every subject (person or idea) will also benefit from manifold embodiment and a plurality of incarnations. To a description of some of those incarnations or forms I now wish to turn. I will not, indeed I cannot, be exhaustive. Thus, I will concentrate on those forms that seem to me most pregnant with the possibility of bringing the imagination to bear on the religious act of teaching: (1) verbal forms, (2) earth forms, (3) embodied forms, (4) forms for discovery. A fifth form, artistic form, will be addressed and exemplified later in chapters 7 and 8.

INCARNATIONAL FORMS FOR TEACHING

VERBAL FORMS

In teaching, the word takes many shapes. The first is the word as metaphor. Concentrating on metaphor reminds us that words are not, initially, abstract concepts. Words are primarily aural sounds, created as symbols for something else. Fundamentally, all words are metaphors. In using words, poets and myth-makers search for the richest and most textured words, and artistically start from the perception that *how* we know is determined by the material with which we know. The approach to knowing that is the way of reasoning moves from data to hypotheses to conclusions, concentrating on idea, concept, and skill—although the hypothesis element in itself is more in the area of hunch and intuition. Often, however, when one begins to stress imagination or intuition, the notion is subtly conveyed that this is better or more valuable than presenting concepts or ideas or thoughts in abstract form. In no way is that a notion I wish to support. But I do want to stress for teachers the hope that in their teaching, equal importance be given to the *vehicle* chosen to express the idea as is given the idea itself. I emphasize this because I am convinced that the vehicle embodies the idea, and form is the shape of content.

For example, I can say to you that I feel like "a phoenix risen from the ashes." Or I can tell you, "I had a hard time, but now things are better." The question is: Would you understand me the same way? I can say, "She is a peach," or I can say, "She is a garden." Would you know *her* the same way? I can say, "I have a mental block." Or I can name my sense of fruitlessness with Wordsworth's description of those times when my mind is like an underground river, lost somewhere in the deep earth, leaving me momentarily dry, but also leaving me hoping it will emerge again with freshness. Again, would you understand me the same way? And more, how would I understand myself?

Many teachers who work with young people are very attentive to the issue of verbal form. They notice with alarm how widespread the life-denying and violent metaphor is in our society, especially in our youth culture. People speak of being "burned out," "wiped out," "blown away," "shattered," "wasted." These examples evoke for us one of the most disturbing characteristics of metaphor today: the dominance of mechanical, machine-like terms and the use of nonhuman imagery and symbol rather than the richer, organic human metaphors. In an extraordinarily prescient passage, William Blake speaks of the impact of mechanical metaphor on our knowing: "Bacon and Newton, sheath'd in dismal steel their terror hang/Like iron scourges over Albion." Iron scourges! If we want to know the power of that metaphor to influence, suggests Elizabeth Sewell, all we need imagine is an intercontinental ballistic missile with an atomic warhead as a kind of self-understanding, sheathed in steel, impending over humanity.[4]

The preponderance of such metaphors places an obligation on the teacher who would use words with reverence: to examine and pay attention to—indeed, to tend carefully—her or his own metaphors. If one's work is to give form through speech, it is more than an arbitrary choice to find words for the form-giving. The choice becomes what I can only call a moral duty. The implications of our words are that important. But tending to verbal forms also obliges us to search out what we can of imaginative uses of language. To take one example, we need to explore Wheelwright's distinctions between "steno-language" and "expressive language."[5] We also need to know what Langer means when she distinguishes between discursive and presentational forms.[6] And we need to be familiar with the kinds of examplars or models offered in the realm of synectics, where one has a choice of several metaphors.[7]

Among these several metaphors, the first is the personal metaphor, the play of "being the thing," where whatever is being studied or addressed is given a first-person opportunity to speak. Dickens, for example, used it to great advantage. We all can imagine what Christmas Past looks like. In another, striking example, Robert Samples remarks how

during and after World War II, U.S. air force officials were astounded at the incredible ease with which Eskimos became skilled maintenance workers on sophisticated aircraft. As their acuity was examined, it became obvious that the Eskimos thought of the aircraft as being alive. They acknowledged circulatory systems, nervous systems, and all the rest. They approached their work in a mystical reverie about the object to which they ministered their "healing."[8]

The personal metaphor is also one of the great powers in Ira Progoff's intensive journaling technique, which is beautifully designed to give us forms for our bodies, our work, and our past to speak.[9] Borrowing from Progoff's insight, I have learned in teaching teaching that a most fruitful opportunity exists when we ask our own teaching to speak.

A second metaphor available to us is the "compressed conflict" or "book title" metaphor: a two-word phrase that captures both the essence of and a paradox involved in the particular thing being studied. Here we might use phrases such as "arbitrary harmony," "expected astonishment," "habitual revelation," "familiar surprise," "demanding satisfier." The point in this play with words is the attempt to bring together two apparently unrelated metaphors and discover likeness between them (the compositive imagination at work).[10] How, for example, is a tire going flat similar to a telegram? What does "hidden brilliance" describe? or "dead birth?" or "transparent curtain"? Having discovered such likenesses, what then can be said of the subject under study?

Perhaps the most powerful metaphor is the simplest, the comparative metaphor or direct analogy. If we think of the teachers who have influenced us most, over and over we are mindful of some example, some image, some use of a comparative metaphor that enabled us to see an entire area of reality. Describing her teacher, Robert Palmer, Rosemary Radford Ruether tells one such story.

It was Palmer, the believing pagan, who first taught me to think theologically or, as he would have called it "mythopoetically." Through him I discovered the meaning of religious symbols, not as extrinsic doctrines, but as living metaphors of human existence. I still remember the great excitement I felt in freshman Humanities when he said something that made me realize that "death and resurrection" was not just some peculiar statement about something that was supposed to have happened to someone 2000 years ago, with no particular connection to anyone else's life. Rather it was a metaphor for inner transformation and rebirth, the mystery of renewed life. He happened to be talking about Attis or Dionysos, not about Jesus. For the first time I understood a new orientation to Christian symbols that eleven years of Catholic education had never suggested to me.[11]

Plato's allegory of the Cave is a comparative metaphor. Heidegger's great myth of Care is another. But comparative metaphors are not always so grand. Evidence this one from baseball.

A player stands at home, dressed in very peculiar clothing, and facing odds of 9 to 1. The future holds a number of possibilities, all difficult. One is that the player will be found "out" or even worse, out of the game. Another is the need for sacrifice. Still another is that the player may be reduced to stealing. And even if there is a positive outcome, it will certainly involve running for one's life, facing down in the earth, covered with dirt, perhaps twisting an ankle, but always straining so that the back bends and the arms are always aching and the sweat runs down the face. And the sun burns, or the rains come, but even if the game is called, it will start again tomorrow.

And why? Why go through all this?

In order to return home.

Comparative metaphors are the heart of verbal form. The repertoire of every imaginative teacher needs them in abundance.

EARTH FORMS

We are human knowers not only through metaphor in verbal form, not only through ideas and concepts put into words. We also know through the world itself, through concrete sensible realities such as sound, stone, wood, fire, and incense. In using the term *earth forms* here, I draw attention to those forms offered to us by the world itself, by the earth that is our mother and our home.

Earth forms teach in and through materiality, which makes a kind of first-level, and indeed mutual claim on us through our own materiality: our bodies and our senses. The third set of forms I will address (embodied forms) also depend on our bodily capacities, but here I want to draw attention not to our receptive learning capacities, but to the earth's concrete teaching capacities.

Wise men and women of all earthly tribes, mythmakers and shamans, gurus and rabbis, storytellers and sculptors, artists and liturgists, have always taught through the stuff of the world itself. They know that our senses are geared to learn from it.

We were talking about my interest in knowledge; but as usual, we were on two different tracks. I was referring to academic knowledge that transcends experience, while he was talking about direct knowledge of the world.

"Do you know anything about the world around you?" he asked.

"I know all kinds of things," I said.

"I mean, do you ever feel the world around you?"

"I feel as much of the world around me as I can."

"That's not enough. You must feel everything, otherwise the world loses its sense."[12]

The implications of this kind of understanding for teaching

are probably apparent. Although prestige is generally given to thinking and learning through conceptual forms, our human organisms persist—despite what we tell them is important—on learning through the material the earth itself presents. If we make verbal forms and earth forms companions in the teaching process, therefore, we are immeasurably enriched. We realize that the stuff of earth has its own life. We come again to reverence the earth, our teacher, who helps us learn what it is to be of the earth.

"Where do I get my forms from?" asks artist Naum Gabo.

I find them everywhere around me, where and when I want to see them. I find them, if I put my mind to it, in a torn piece of cloud carried away by the wind. I can find them in the naked stones on hills and roads. I see them in the green thicket of leaves and trees. I may discern them in a steamy trail of smoke from a passing train or on the surface of a shabby wall. Their apparition may be sudden, it may come and vanish in a second, but when they are over, they leave me with the image of eternity's duration.[13]

To know grass and glass, wind and smoke, stone and sound, wood and wine as our teachers is to begin to repair broken relations, relations hurt by the false notions that our first relation to earth is to dominate and that whatever is, is ours alone.

Every imaginative teacher should be familiar with the broad repertoire of earth forms in order to utilize them in teaching. Although that repertoire is vast, it may be illustrated through four basic forms. Each of these forms takes its name from one of the elements basic to the earth itself: water, earth, fire, and air.

The first basic earth form to incorporate into teaching is *water*. The imaginative teacher can use any situation where water is central. This can mean ocean coast, seashore or lakeshore. It can mean rain whether gentle, violent, sudden, or expected. It can mean any time when one is washing: hands before meals, the body before the day begins or at its end. It can mean the washing of the bodies of the very old, the very young. It can mean the water of human tears. Teachers might use rainy days as catalysts for understanding water with their students, but they need not wait for such occasions. One of the reasons plants and flowers are often present in the learning environment is that they enhance the environment. More powerful, because it is more subtle, is the need for water in such cases. A teacher might draw attention to the need for water to keep plants alive and flowers fresh. Without water, there is death.

The second basic earth form is *earth* itself, in all its manifestations: dirt, clay, mud, ground, soil, desert, rocks, hills, valleys, mountains. The form, *earth*, also includes images that describe its sheltering of us: the ground on which we stand, the burial place of our foremothers and forefathers, the spinning planet groaning—as does all creation—in expectation of what we are to do to it and to be with it. Earth also reminds us of relationship(s): earth, the planet we share with almost five billion others; earth, the parent and teacher holding us as we sleep and receiving us when we wake; earth, the intimate we have failed so often, but which has not as yet failed us.

Native Americans have never lost this rich sense of earth. It is eloquently expressed in the 1854 address of Chief Seattle to an assembly of tribes preparing to sign treaties: "Every part of this earth is sacred to my people. Every shining pine needle, every sandy shore, every mist in the dark woods, every clearing and humming insect is holy in the memory and experience of my people." For Chief Seattle, the teaching to be done out of this conviction was clear.

You must teach your children that the ground beneath their feet is the ashes of our ancestors. So that they will respect the land, tell your children that the earth is rich with the lives of our kin. Teach your children what we have taught our children, that the earth is our mother. Whatever befalls the earth befalls the children of the earth. To spit upon the ground is to spit upon themselves. This we know. The earth does not belong to the people; the people belong to the earth. This we know. All things are connected like blood which unites one family.[14]

The third basic earth form that we should incorporate into teaching is *fire*. For most of the inhabitants of earth, fire is for heat, light, protection, and cooking. Religious rituals have always drawn on its power to banish darkness, to offer sacrifice, to signal the presence and the place of the sacred. Thus, lighting candles before a religious service and extinguishing them at its end are ways of saying, "Remember, you are on holy ground." It might be to our advantage to begin the teaching situation (as we often do at special mealtimes) by lighting a candle. The fire can serve as a symbol not only of the teacher's intention to enlighten the minds and spirits of others, but more importantly to symbolize, "Here, *too*, you are on holy ground."

The final basic earth form is one without which we could not speak: *air* or wind or breath or spirit. The physical, personal aspect of teaching demands that we use speech, draw breath before one another. Oxygen, in amounts tolerable to the human organism, is essential if we hope to learn. Indeed, many elementary-school teachers draw students' attention to the need for air or breath through physical exercises: "Class please stand! Hands on shoulders. Now, breathe in. Breathe out. One, two. Three, four." I also know of one graduate school professor of theology who draws breath regularly with her class. And many other teachers begin teaching sessions with a moment of silence, not in order to pray, but in order to incorporate air as ally into the teaching act.

To my mind, the importance of these earth forms is manifold. They are the milieu in which we dwell as we teach. A distinction may be made between *thinking about* and *being in* something, but a separation is impossible. Teaching, at its best, is a bringing together of the two: *thinking about* that in which we *are* every moment of our waking lives. Therefore, at a first level, it is crucial for us to come to terms with the water, earth, fire, and air that give us bodily life. At a second level, the primordial character of earth forms as companions to us in human life, accompanying us daily, reminds us of our basic relatedness not only to one another, but to all being. Earth forms are basic symbols. How we address, handle, and touch them grounds the way we address, handle, and touch more manufactured, artificial things: books, pencils, chalk, oil, tea, ointment, floors, clocks, bells. The list is endless, but the archetypal or sacramental character of the earth form stands. Teaching is always done through the mediation of a third—a third, which, like clay, breath, fire, and tears, is often of the earth.

Further, earth forms are reminders of the primary places where teaching takes place: in communities of people, especially in families; in work, athletics, and artistic environments; in both spontaneous and in consciously planned situations. School teaching at its best is always a limit, a boundary example of human teaching. And although earth forms may not always be the stuff of every classroom, they are the stuff of every life.

Finally, earth forms continually recur in the spirituality of religious peoples and are central to all religious ritual. Whether one speaks of *prana*, the goodness in the air one breathes; of candles, whose flames one lights in preparation for Shabbat; of spittle mixed with earth, whose touch gave sight to the blind in the miracles of Jesus; the Spirit of God breathing over the waters and causing creation; or the Spirit of God arriving in Pentecostal tongues of fire: A *religious* consciousness is one that sees the holiness in things, the sacred in things, and the teaching capacity in things of the earth.

Dorothea Soelle tells of a pious old man in his last years who, though sound in mind, was feeble in speech. All the old man could say—and he said it repeatedly—was " 'Everything, everything, everything.' He died with these words on his lips. This word is a kind of formula, a symbol for the confirmation of totality . . . the kind of piety that affirms everything, omits and forgets nothing and no one."[15] It is also a formula both for the wisdom which knows that nothing which exists is without the capacity to teach, and for the piety demanded by those who relate to others as teacher.

EMBODIED FORMS

In his brilliant book/essay, *The Metaphoric Mind*, Robert Samples speaks of several human modes, each of which are metaphoric. He calls them mindscapes. Samples calls one the "integrative metaphoric." He says that it occurs when the physical and psychic attributes of people are extended into direct experience with objects, processes, and conditions outside themselves. The integrative metaphoric mode requires what Samples calls "getting into it."[16] When I speak of *embodied forms*—the third type of form a subject may take that allows us to bring the imagination to bear on the religious act of teaching—such physical and psychic interchange is critical. As forms for teaching, embodied forms are those where the teaching is shaped in a way that requires both the physical *and* the psychic involvement of the entire person. Of course, by the very fact of being in the world, one is physically present. But here I am speaking of teaching forms where bodiliness is the means and the stuff of teaching. Sensory absorption is the key, whether it is touching, tasting, imitating, hearing, or dramatizing whatever is confronted. If the absorption is to be complete, however, it must be more than physical. Indeed, at first it may not apparently *be* physical, in the sense that such absorption is evident to someone watching. The absorption may be entirely contemplative, or it may happen in the mode of the reflective observer.

If teaching *is* the incarnation of subject matter, then the life and death of every kind of subject in all the meaning of the term subject, is teaching's appropriate concern. Since human beings (teachers) are the primary and most compelling embodied forms, we must not deny that all people in the teaching situation, by their very presence, are teaching what it means to be human, what it means to live and die.

As part of a program at a school where I taught, I once was asked to spend an evening sharing my "spiritual journey" with the community. As I prepared, I felt that I wanted to shape the presentation of my life as a myth, but that thought seemed to border on the arrogant. Upon reflection with my wise philosopher friend Joanmarie Smith, however, I realized that my instinct was grounded in human experience, an experience some of our greatest poets and teachers have explored. I realized that everyone's life is mythic. Such was the great insight of Goethe, and it is the primary reason we are drawn to drama, to the novel, to biography. We have a human sense that each of our lives can reveal something of life to another. We have a sense that when we are asked, "How did you get to be the way you are?" the question is not one of voyeurism or of intrusion. It is the question, "Where does your life speak to me about my life?" or "What can your life say about mine?"

Even when the question is not asked verbally or consciously, it is in the air. Children try to get the knack of being human by watching their parents, other adults, and their peers. And although the term "role model" may be overused, from the beginning the human race has been learning the nature of human subjectivity by observing others in all the roles they play. Further, because our humanness includes our sexuality, we teach not only the meaning of life and death, but the meaning of sexuality as well. We answer the questions, "What is it to be a woman? What is it to be a man?" not with one answer, but because of our variedness, with innumerable answers. If incarnation (embodiment) is at the center of teaching, so, too, is sexuality and the mystery sexuality symbolizes concerning human need, human attraction, and human completeness.

Although human beings may be the primary embodied forms, embodied form does not refer to human beings alone. The physical and psychic involvement it calls for extends to the other elements in creation as well as to us. Indeed, no subject matter exists that is not amenable to being learned in and through bodily involvement. Children know this better than most adults. For example, watch a child becoming fully engaged with food.

Peas. Mash into thin sheet on plate. Press back of fork into peas. Hold fork vertically, prongs up, and lick off peas.
Mashed Potatoes: Pat mashed potatoes flat on top. Dig several little depressions. Think of them as ponds or pools. Fill pools with gravy. With fork, sculpt rivers between pools and watch the gravy flow between them. Decorate with peas. Do not eat. Alternate method: Make a large hole in center of mashed potatoes. Pour in ketchup. Stir until potatoes turn pink. Eat as you would peas.
Ice-cream cone: Ask for double scoop. Knock the top scoop off while walking out door of the ice-cream parlor. Cry. Lick remaining scoop slowly so that ice cream melts down outside of the cone and over your hand. Stop licking when ice cream is even with top of cone. Eat a hole in bottom of cone and suck the rest of ice cream out the bottom. When only cone remains with ice cream coating the inside, leave on car dashboard.[17]

The point of these examples should not be missed. They illustrate brilliantly children's capacity to become involved with subject matter through the full range of their bodiliness. They also illustrate the kind of activity embodied form implies.

FORMS FOR DISCOVERY

In naming this last set of forms, I want to complete the set offered in this chapter (artistic forms will be dealt with in chapters 7 and 8), and to anticipate the theme of chapter 4. When I speak of forms for discovery, or discovering, I refer to ways of teaching that are designed without a particular end in view; without knowledge of what will occur as a result; and which, *in the design itself*, are planned in such a way that new, and often unsuspected, understanding is made manifest. The religious term for this is revelation.

Forms for discovery are characteristically set up in order to "see what happens"; this is their *purpose*. Where instruction in tennis is directed toward playing tennis, instruction in Greek toward learning Greek, and instruction in history toward learning history, discovered forms are, as the name suggests, directed toward finding out whatever is there to be found, without prejudging the outcome. I am aware of, indeed I celebrate, the presence of this characteristic in all learning. More, I hope it would always be present. But in forms for discovery, I wish to emphasize this as the *purpose* of the form, not merely an accident or by-product of the learning process.

Proper to a form for discovery is the design of a situation. Stand on a street corner and give away flowers; spend three days in a strange city with only a dollar in your pocket; pose as a visitor from another country or as a person from a different religion or social class. These are all forms for discovery, and their only limits are the imaginations of the persons involved. My own experience of the beauty of this form was solidified several years ago in a class on clowning from a course called "The Aesthetic and Religious Education." I will describe the course in some detail later in this book, but the following example is pertinent here.

The time was just before Christmas, and the leader that day was Carol Brink. After a brief verbal explanation in which she reminded us of the nonverbal, symbolic, and nonrational aspects of the clown, we were directed to dress in baggy clothes and to paint one another's faces with the white mask of death over which we traced the superimposed features of new life.

Then we were directed to leave the safety of our classroom, to go out in twos and threes, and to do something foolish, risking ourselves in the midst of a serious academic day, on a serious academic campus. Most of us chose to give away money, food, fruit, and candy (we had some Hershey Kisses and some Tootsie Rolls). When the food ran out, we gave away silent blessings by placing our hands on the heads of people we met. The children we encountered knew us instantly (in Heschel's phrase, they "knew what they saw" rather than "seeing what they knew"[18]). They were not surprised by clowns on campus, and they were *able* to be surprised by clowns on campus. Workers on the grounds knew us, too, as did the vice president for development. When told, "The clowns are here, but they're not talking," he responded, "Not with words, they're not."

But there was no way to assess our impact on others—that had not been our intention—only to share the poignancy, the silence, the newness, and the discovery with one another. For that reason it was peculiarly revelatory, indeed a true "discovering," to receive two days later a letter from an older student we had met and blessed. The letter read:

> Dear Wednesday Afternoon Fools:
>
> Your smiling, funny faces
> Found in unexpected places
> Have brought a wondrous brightness to my day.
> And the Tootsie Roll you gave me
> Though it maybe didn't save me
> It helped me one more step along the way.
>
> The season here is lonely,
> And I believe that only
> Those who live it can relate to what I mean.
> Every "blessed" thing is URGENT—
> Papers, finals, church-school pageant—
> And the Advent/Christmas meaning leaves the scene.
>
> But you walked through a doorway,
> And instead of blocking your way,
> I received a tiny present that you found.
> And your silent, clownish blessing
> Has led me to confessing

That I went away with feet "on higher ground."

Marcia

I tell this story because it describes so well the possibilities that exist in forms of discovery, and because we do not always find out, as we did after that Wednesday afternoon, what is possible when one sets out to learn. I also tell it as a metaphor for what happens whenever teaching is at its best. The incarnation of the subject matter makes subject matter present in such a way that the outcome is revelation. Let us now explore revelation as fundamental to the concept of teaching as an activity of religious imagination.

4. Revelation

This chapter draws on the imagery of revelation found in everyday speech, in theology, and in pedagogy in order to facilitate understanding the teaching act as one of religious imagination. I will begin by describing several revelatory moments and by probing possible meanings of revelation. Then I will move to the central issue of the chapter, how the revelation of subject matter is fostered in teaching. I will conclude by responding to the questions, "Toward what is the revelation directed?"

REVELATORY MOMENTS

I have proposed that teaching is the incarnation of subject matter, in such a way that it leads to the revelation of subject matter. In responding to the question, "What does that look like?" we have already encountered a number of moments of revelation in the course of this text: Rosemary Radford Ruether's "moment of great excitement" in Robert Palmer's class, which made her "realize"; the lieutenant's discovery that the map used successfully by his troops was of the Pyrenees, not the Alps; Helen Keller's understanding of w-a-t-e-r; Eliza Doolittle's correct pronunciation of "rain"; and Kazantzakis's protagonist, looking at the dead butterfly in his hand. Each of these shares a particular kind of description: Keller's, "I knew then; a thrill of returning thought; awakened my soul"; Henry Higgins's, "She's got it; by George, she's got it"; Ruether's, "For the first time I understood." All describe the process of revelation. Worley on Van Doren provides another example: "It must unfold as grace, inevitably, necessarily, as tomcats stretch. . . . " So, too, does Eliot: It is an "unattended moment," one so deep the music is not heard at all, "but you *are* the music . . . "; and Kazantzakis: "It is a law not to be violated, an eternal rhythm."

Only the rare human being does not remember moments of

such revelation in her or his own life. Only the rare teacher has not incarnated subject matter in such a way. If we want to understand the meaning of revelation as intrinsic to the teaching process, it is wise to stop here—or, if working with apprentice teachers, to invite them to do so—and reflect on the embodiments of such moments in our own lives. One of my most contemplative students, Art Kubick, recognized the form revelation took in his life after completing his doctorate: "On this second half of the journey, learning is not so much a discovering of something completely new as a reencountering of old friends, a deepening of beliefs already held." In all of the above resides a sense of the unfolding of mystery in time, slowly or swiftly, a reverence for gradual growth, as well as a capacity to be suffused by wonder and surprised by joy in an instant.

THREE MEANINGS OF REVELATION

Having taken time to reflect on revelatory experiences, we can move to the question, "What meanings of revelation underlie these experiences?" In other words, what *is* the meaning of revelation? This question may be explored from several perspectives. A universal, archetypal, or sacramental meaning of revelation is present in everyday speech. We use the term *revelation* to name something disclosed, uncovered, unveiled. The moment of revelation is characterized by knowing as coming-to-know, often by a sudden "I see!" (And, of course, what you see is what you get.) Revelation is a source of enlightenment, a disclosing of something previously unknown or not realized. A reality has been before our eyes—we have been looking at it, but have not as yet seen it. Often, to pursue a point alluded to above,

What impairs our sight are habits of seeing as well as the mental concomitants of seeing. Our sight is suffused with knowing, instead of feeling painfully the lack of knowing what we see. The principle to be kept in mind is to know what we see rather than to see what we know.[1]

In other cases we do not see because the form (the embodiment, the incarnation) and the *moment* have not come together. Of particular interest to teachers may be the notion that, in common understanding, revelation is always a form of knowledge, characteristically brought to view and exposed through discourse and communication. Initially, however, I simply want to point out that revelation is *not* basically a theological or Christian word, but one commonly used in everyday speech.

At the same time, revelation *is* a word central to theology and religion, and its meaning in these contexts may illuminate what teaching is about. Gabriel Moran's groundbreaking work on the religious meaning of revelation has enormous implications. He writes in several places that revelation is not, as often thought, a body of truths, a deposit, a record—even the biblical record itself. Instead, the starting point for understanding revelation as a religious or theological concept is a divinity revealing itself to human beings who are conscious, receptive, listening, attending subjects. The revelation of this divinity, often known as unknown, or as Unnameable and Unspeakable Mystery, is mediated through events or persons or communities or things or words, indeed, through an entire revelatory creation. But that through which the revelatory process occurs is not the primary focus; it plays the essential but secondary role of mediation.[2]

To put it in a slightly different way, revelation is a process with two main elements, but these are not the divinity and divinely revealed truths, events, or insights. Rather, the two main elements in revelation are the divinity revealing and humans listening and responding. Revelation is a *relation* between subjects, knowing subjects. Revelation is a meeting between persons. Revelation is what happens in the "in between" of personal relationships. "The reality is the relation; the meeting is the revelation."[3] This also means that revelation is present and social. "Persons reveal, and it is persons who are revealed; through being persons they reveal, and through revealing they become persons."[4]

From this perspective, if one asks, even within the context of theological teaching on revelation, *"What is revealed?"* the entire tradition of Christian theology teaches that it is the Ultimate which is revealed, or more comprehensively, the direct object of the verb *reveal* is divinity/humanity/reality. Instead of saying Christianity or Judaism or Buddhism or the Bible *has* a revelation, it is more correct to say Christianity or Judaism or Buddhism or the Bible *is* a revelation, or in personal terms, a community of people engaged in and becoming aware of a disclosure of Being in the present. (And of a disclosure of beings-in-the-present, revelation's social and relational component.) This points finally to the reality that revelation is temporal, and that it is occurring *now* or not at all in the fleshly, individual, communal lives of children and adults. Possibly, it is occurring as well in the nonhuman and animal worlds too; in all of the earth forms.

Even from this cursory description, the reader will realize some of the implications of such an understanding for teaching: the primacy of relational life; the multiform idea of Subject Matter suggested in the understanding of the *what* that is revealed as the Divine Mystery/human beings/universe; the appropriateness of all elements in creation as forms for incarnating subject matter; and the gradual coming to know in time. Teaching understood as the revealing of subject matter through the incarnation of subject matter is perfectly consonant with revelation as a religious doctrine. The doctrine is sacramental, archetypal, that is, an expression of religious imagination.

In addition to the everyday and the theological meanings of revelation, a third meaning exists, embedded in educational thought. Allow me several examples. In *On Knowing*, Jerome Bruner proposes the following hypothesis:

I shall operate on the assumption that discovery, whether by a schoolboy going it on his own or by a scientist cultivating the growing edge of her field, is in its essence a matter of rearranging or transforming evidence in such a way that one is enabled to go beyond the evidence so assembled to new insights. It may well be that an additional fact or shred of evidence makes this larger transformation possible. But it is often not even dependent on new information.[5]

In other words, revelation cannot be guaranteed. At the same time, however, it *can* be witnessed:

The teacher, as has been recognized at least since Plato's MENO, is not primarily someone who knows instructing someone who does not know. [The teacher] is rather someone who attempts to re-create the subject in the student's mind, and [the] strategy in doing this is first of all to get the student to recognize what the student already potentially knows ... That is why it is the teacher rather than the student, who asks most of the questions.[6]

But teachers, paradoxically, also evoke the possibility of revelation by refusing to answer questions. Evidence the following example from one such teacher.

Student: "If the Buddha is more than Siddhartha Gotama, who lived many centuries ago, then tell me, please, what is the real nature of Buddha?"

Teacher: "The blossoming branch of a plum tree."

Student: "What I asked, worthy sir, and what I am eager to know is, What is the Buddha?"

Teacher: "A pink fish with golden fins swimming idly through the blue sea."

Student: "Will not your reverence tell me what the Buddha is?"

Teacher: "The full moon, cold and silent in the night sky, turning the dark meadow to silver."[7]

Roger Hazelton, commenting on the student-teacher relation in the above example, reports that such is the dialogue in its entirety. "We are not told whether the student went to the bursar's office to get his tuition money back. Is this any way to treat an eager learner?"[8] But then Hazelton goes on to reflect on the nature of the interaction as revelation:

But suppose the Zen master, for all his seeming evasiveness, really wanted to show his pupil that he had asked an unanswerable sort of question. The nature of the Buddha is not a neutral, public fact to be defined in commonsense terms. Quite the contrary; it has to do with the kind of blessed reality that is open only to an alert, deeply personal responsiveness. So a student would do better to begin by attending more closely and feelingly to the rich detail and amazing variety of the world disclosed in his own experience, real or imagined. Plum blossoms, idling fish, or a cold full moon are more than data to be ticked off and filed away under abstract categories. They are, or may become, eye-openers that sharpen one's awareness of a livelier, larger reality beneath the surfaces of things. Then looking becomes seeing, and seeing becomes believing.[9]

Such is the "stuff" of revelation: eye-openers; the world disclosed in experience, real or imagined; awareness of reality beneath the surfaces of things; verbal forms; earth forms; embodied forms; forms of discovery.

Then looking becomes seeing, seeing becomes believing, and learning becomes revelation.

A final example. William Walsh, professor of education at the University of Leeds, offers one of the most insightful and poetic descriptions of teaching and revelation I know. He asserts there is always more than the psychological dimension in learning:

[Learning] is always something *revealed* as well as something performed. Learning as revelation is an idea with Platonic and Christian vibrations which may for some be sufficient to make it unwelcome. But however much these grate . . . it is important for the teacher to realize that it contains at least an unmistakable negative truth, attested by daily experience. *Learning cannot be guaranteed.* To believe that it can, even with every circumstance and effort cooperating, is to regard humans as infallibly adjusting organisms, teaching as the cunning manipulation of environment, and learning as producing the appropriate reaction in a specific situation. . . . Human dignity requires us to admit the possibility of failure. The vocation of teacher involves a sense of reverence in the presence of mystery, the role of learner entails patience and stillness in waiting on the event. Learning should begin in wonder, go on in humility and end in gratitude. And gratitude is a feeling in place only in the presence of something given. It is the correlate of Grace.[10]

TEACHING: FOSTERING THE REVELATION OF SUBJECT MATTER

It should now be apparent that the kind of knowing revelation suggests is not accomplished by handing over subject matter, by retailing information, and certainly not by telling someone who does not "know" something that the teacher "knows." The revelation of subject matter I am proposing is better approached by exercising a "negative capability"—a phrase Keats used of Shakespeare to illustrate the capacity for living in uncertainties, mystery, and doubt, without irritably searching after fact and reason. One who would foster revelation must take on all the roles in the house of religious imagination: contemplative (explorer of darkness and silence), ascetic (professing rigor and detachment), creator (reforming with ontological tenderness), sacrament (alert to the presence of mystery everywhere, any-where, nowhere). One must take an approach not of direct, but of indirect communication.

INDIRECT COMMUNICATION

I believe that indirect communication is the central route to be taken by teachers who understand their work as one of religious imagination; by teachers who want to foster revelation. The phrase, *indirect communication*, is best known for its use by Sören Kierkegaard. Because his work is so fruitful for teaching, I will draw heavily on Kierkegaard and use him as a starting point. Then I will try to show where his work leads and what original insights it might produce for teaching today, especially as it speaks to the core of teaching: the "raising of the question."

As Sara Little points out in her gem-like book on teaching, *To Set One's Heart,* the term *indirect communication* is almost tech-nically owned by Kierkegaard, so closely is it associated with him.[11] Nonetheless, I hope it will be more universally claimed. To achieve this, I find the twenty-year-old analysis of James Whitehill most helpful, for it extends Kierkegaard's work and applies it in other contexts. Whitehill lifts from Kierkegaard

The Elements of Indirect Communication

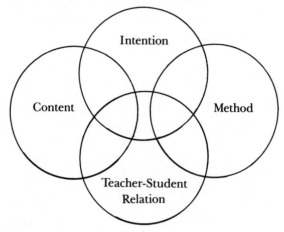

Intention

Content

Method

Teacher-Student
Relation

four aspects of communication: intention, content, method, and the relationship of communicator and receiver.[12]

Intention

With reference to intention, the role of imagination is critical. What teachers imagine they are doing—what they assume they are doing, what they think they are doing, what they *intend* to do—pervades, colors, and determines what they do, in fact, do. Kierkegaard first speaks about intention in order to disabuse his hearers (who thought themselves Christians) of the illusion they were Christians, to disabuse them of the illusion they could "know" the divinity. Kierkegaard states that when the communicator faces the hearer, the communicator's purpose or intent must be to confront the hearer (receiver of the communication) in a way that enables the hearer to discover that a rigorous demand is set before her or him. That demand, in Kierkegaard's words, is an "existence possibility" that impels the hearer to choose whether her or his relationship toward the communication will be a positive or a negative one. In so doing, the hearer chooses his or her own *subjectivity*. In other words, the hearer is not asked to choose for or against the possibility offered—that is, the subject matter as a "system of clues." Rather, the hearer is asked to choose what relation she or he will have *toward* that possibility (subject matter). The hearer makes this choice, says Kierkegaard, through a double reflection: through apprehension of the form presented, and through appropriation of the form in relationship to the self.

If we substitute the words teacher and student for communicator and hearer, we see that the teacher's intention is to try to arouse the student's capacity to make a choice. Kierkegaard calls this an ethical capacity, because it is one where freedom and choice in the hearer (student) become active; and Kierkegaard says that the teacher wants this capacity to become active, intends to make the learner self-active, choosing herself or himself in self-knowledge and subjectivity. The teacher's intention can thus be viewed as at least fourfold, directed toward:

1. awakening thought
2. creating tension

3. arousing ethical response
4. opening a communion of subjectivity

This analysis could be read as a brief *against* direct communication, where the teacher intends to deliver content in the form of facts or information. Remember, however, that such intention can always have beneath it the issue *why* the delivering of content is engaged in; namely, what the teacher *imagines* will happen as a result of her or his communication. Put another way, the relation of direct and indirect communication may be one of partners rather than of opposites.

We can find in our culture many exemplars of such a rendering of intention, consonant with a theory of indirect communication. We see in teachers like the following the discipline and distance of the ascetic imagination at work. Martin Buber begs other teachers to work "as if you did not" and reminds us that we fail the student if the communication is offered with a gesture of interference.[13] Sylvia Ashton-Warner instructs Maori children in New Zealand to create their own books, thus their own reality.[14] Seonaid Robertson brings art to children and adolescents in the hope its stimulus will startle them into new awareness.[15] Paulo Freire educates for critical consciousness, especially among the very poor.[16] The past, too, is filled with reports of such teachers: Jesus, Buddha, Mohammed, and Moses.

My point in citing these teachers is to refute the notion that indirect communication is only one of many methods of teaching, only one way of going about the forming of intention. Rather, the kind of intention resident in indirect communication must be found in *all* teaching. No matter what the subject matter, the teacher is trying to embody form in a way that helps the learner discover a relationship to that subject. The relation then issues in a demand made, a choice offered, a course of action proposed. If teaching occurs in a situation where there is radical respect for the other's freedom and choice, the other will quite possibly be able to discover a power within to respond to a demand, to make a choice, to initiate an action. The learner's response may be positive or it may be negative; but once acted upon, the circuit (learning circle) is completed. The learner (receiver) touches a power within the self, a power arising out of her or his own subjectivity, a capacity and ability to act or not to act.

Thus the teacher's fourfold intention becomes alive in the student. First, thought awakens—the student feels the thrill of returning thought. Second, tension is created: the student feels herself or himself pushed away from the status quo and prodded—sometimes impelled in a nonrational way—from comfort to discomfort. (Buber goes so far as to say the test of the educator *lies* in conflict with the pupil).[17] Third, deep in the student a conviction is aroused: not only to *do* something (or be something, or dream something, or await something, or allow something to happen) but to recognize that one is morally, ethically, religiously *called* to do something. Finally, the student has—*sees*—an existence possibility. If the student does respond, she or he finds revealed more than her or his own subjectivity. The student finds that she or he is involved in a communion of subjectivity with that which has been made present—presented—to the student. This is what a teacher, in terms of indirect communication hopes for; this is what a teacher, in terms of indirect communication, intends.

Content

Such intention assumes a special relation to content, the second aspect of indirect communication. In a direct communication, it is relatively easy to have an image of content. As a teacher, I have facts, information, theory, ideas, data, or procedures in my mind. I have skills to be demonstrated by my body (for example, skating or violin playing). My students and I can both see and check the content with one another to decide whether it corresponds. Much of teaching, perhaps all of it, must necessarily assume this image in the beginning, and no reason exists why it should not. Our world could not run without a specific and technical vision of content. To stop here, however, to so limit our vision, is to fail. For if our intention is to help others claim their own power (*their* existence possibilities, their subjectivity in communion) and to foster the revelation of subject matter, then beneath all such technical imagery teachers need to see content as essentially elusive, ambiguous, and in the realm of mystery—that about which we can never know everything. Content is a medium for something deeper. In direct communication, we can generally muster enough clarity to avoid misunderstanding and to ensure the absence of error as far as possible. But, in indirect communication, the content will be more. It will differ not only insofar as each subject's uniqueness, but also because the deepest knowledge, as every child can explain, is that where "I know but I can't say." The religious imagination, almost by definition, stands as advocate for a fullness of content as knowledge entered, knowledge embodied, knowledge in which people dwell. It stands for mystery. It stands for the apophatic, for ambiguity, for paradox. And it stands in darkness "in this, my half-rest" where

> Knowing slows for a moment,
> And not-knowing enters, silent,
> Bearing being itself . . . [18]

Content bearing being itself is content bearing revelation. The delivery occurring is not of content to receivers, *but of receivers to themselves*—as essentially existing, responsible, moral, and religious subjects.

Method

The intention of the teacher is to manifest content in such a way that the content escapes attempts to make it fixed, secure, ordered, understood, and tolerable. At the same time, this content *seduces* into rapt attention. What method will foster this? Surely it evades the question to suggest that the teacher simply tries to be as obscure as possible (although I stand willing to appreciate that some might make this charge of what I am saying).

Chapter 3 offered a partial response to the aspect of method by naming and discussing the incarnation of form: verbal, earth, embodied, discovered. I now add to this category an entire range of activities such as the use of masks, incognito, irony, humor, asides, digressions,[19] and forms of expressive language, such as soft-focus, indirection, the paralogical, and light assertion.[20] Sara Little adds parables, drama, film, silence, introspection.[21] Much of chapters 7 and 8 are devoted to the presence and practice of art as a method or form. In the area of religion, because the knowledge to be conveyed does not easily lend itself to direct utterance, the above are often the only methods of teaching available. Death, life, birth, and suffering—indeed, all the great realities—are essentially beyond discursive speech.

Kierkegaard, however, does give us some further clues concerning method. The first clue is that it is essential for the teacher to go to the "place" where the receiver (student) is located. Again, this demands using the ascetic imagination, taking pains to find where the other is, and beginning there.

All true effort to help begins with self-humiliation; the helper must first humble himself under him he would help, and therewith must understand that to help does not mean to be a sovereign but to be a servant, that to help does not mean to be ambitious but to be patient, that to help means to endure for the time being the imputation that one is in the wrong and does not understand what the other understands.[22]

To my mind this first clue has political ramifications. If we go to the others' place as teachers, this means we go to *all* their places. Learners exist not only in psychic, personal "places"; they exist in physical places as well. Indirect communication can be charged with being elite or esoteric—as can any philosophy—unless teachers address the total environment of the learner as well as the learners themselves. Thus, the vocation to teach involves teaching in particular places. Going to "the place where the learner is" often involves taking into account hard realities: hunger, oppression, poverty, and economic need. Given this, indirect communication might necessarily take forms that lessen injustice: starting food co-ops, offering health services, providing meals, finding jobs.

But when words are chosen to make up an artistic configuration of human life, when words are the form of the existence possibility the teacher offers, those words as formed must be both appropriate to and appropriable by the learner. For example, in the United States, black women are asking for forms other than those where "all the women are white and all the blacks are men."[23] All women are asking or beginning to ask for forms where we do not have to translate from male experience into our own. Asians, Latin Americans, Africans, as well as the people of Oceania, do not live in a NATO world where "the continent" is equivalent to Western Europe, or "America" is equivalent to the United States. The Near East and the Middle East are not east of everywhere on the globe. Forms must have some consonance, some resonance with the learner's experience.

In the special case of teachers of religion, this aspect of method has frightening, yet creative implications. The God who was declared dead in the 1960s *is* dead for many. Appropriate and more appropriable forms to express the nature of the divine-human reality of Subject Matter are desperately needed. A divinity beyond any we have yet imagined may reside at the core of things, waiting to become manifest, and old images of that divinity may need burial. Dead, too, are many of the forms the world's religions have taken, especially those shaped by colonialism and patriarchy. This holds particularly true for those religious visions that appear to dismiss the profound insights of traditions other than their own.

What does this mean for method? Taking the lead from indirect communication in Kierkegaard, we can see that if every aspect of content can be presented "as if it were not," and if the teacher acts "as if she did not," then everything will be able to be approached as a question. It may even be true that the essence of method will become the posing of the question. There will not—indeed, there cannot—be an immediate demand for adherence (to content). Rather, teachers and learners will both come to content as questioners, presenting questions to one another and to subject matter.

And what *are* genuine questions? Are they not probes into reality initiated by knowing a little, and not necessarily found in interrogative form? Are they not issues concerning love, birth, nearness, intimacy, agony, war, disease, evil? Is not even the simplest-appearing subject matter, from simple addition to irregular verbs, related to the comprehensive question which human life itself is? Is not all subject matter an attempt to answer the question, "How do we give form to our world?" Is it not true that a human being is that being in whose being Being is always in question? Does not the nervous or inappropriate laughter that so often accompanies our hearing Hamlet's "To be or not to be; that is the question" stem precisely from our touching bottom, our experience of utter nakedness in the face of existence?

In Zen Buddhism, as we have seen, the teacher is one who exhibits qualifications to teach by brushing questions off with a paradox. To answer a question creates the danger of consolidating the mental level on which the question was asked. Something must be held in reserve, hinting at the possibility of better or more complete existence. Unless this happens, advancement into knowing and not knowing is halted. In *The Color Purple,* Alice Walker eloquently captures this core of teaching, which lies in the posing of the question.

I think us here to wonder, myself. To wonder. To ast. And that in wondering 'bout the big things and asting bout the big things, you learn about the little ones, almost by accident. But you never know nothing more about the big things than you start out with. The more I wonder, he say, the more I love.[24]

My assertion that posing the question is the center of the teaching act is, I believe, critical. One goes to where the other is as a preliminary, as an accompaniment to method. But when one gets there, the activity called for is the raising of, the posing of, and the dwelling with the other together in the presence of, the question.

The Teacher-Student Relation

The last aspect in indirect communication is the relation of teacher and student. Earlier in this chapter, I suggested the need to integrate religious imagination into the work of teaching as revelation. In my view, such integration becomes crucial when we consider the relation of teacher and student. Kierkegaard may be right in seeing the relation as one of confrontation (of teacher as midwife), but I cannot agree that the direction is one of confrontation toward the receiver alone, as if the receiver were standing in essential solitude. I believe that we can view the relation from a richer vantage point.

Instead of viewing the relation as one between two separate, unrelated selves, I believe we can look at it through the lens of religious imagination. Religious imagination can lead to community with one another, sharing in the communion of subjectivity of which I have already spoken. If religious imagination is brought to bear on the relation, the teacher and the student will find they walk *together* on the four imaginative paths.

First, they are *co-contemplatives*. Subject matter stands before them as existence possibility, and the primary attitude of the onlooker (the reflector, the worshiper) is reverence. And yet, teacher and student together are also subjects, thus they also are related to one another as existence possibilities, as Thou. The choice they make regarding the subject matter (viz., themselves), the choice whether their relation will be a negative or positive relation, is a choice to see the other subject and the other's subjectivity as essentially outsider, not-like-me, even as enemy (negative relation), or to see the other as sister or brother (positive relation). This choice begins with contemplation; it is difficult to imagine how any other existence possibilities can be chosen if this primary one is not.

The second relation between teacher and student is *ascetic*. Not only must there be respect in the relation, there must also be a refusal to manipulate, to intrude (as Buber says, one fails as teacher with even the *gesture* of interference), to answer questions the other might answer. Put another way, the teacher and the student *may not use* one another. This ascetic component in teaching ensures that the teacher and student will be looking at what is before them, at the "third" in teaching, and at the knowledge that it—whatever the "third" is—must be approached with discipline, with willingness to wrest meaning from it, with sweat, often with tears, but without violation.

The third relation is one of *co-creation*. Teacher and student must approach one another with a sense of one another's radical novelty. They must bring to bear on the relation the mystical sense, the belief that everything is indeed related to everything else. They must face not only one another, but content, too, as if it had never been seen before (the insight small children forever keep before the rest of us), even while intuiting all kinds of connections. And if questions have been posed in freedom and with respect, the teacher and student will discover the truth that *both*, and not just the teacher, are creator and creative. Subject matter met for the first time lends itself differently when approached by each unique subject, and new existence possibilities are waiting to be discovered and to be created. Aware of the temptation teachers almost always have to arrogate the genuinely creative to themselves, Thomas Merton used to borrow from Sufi writers to warn novices to avoid as masters

> Those who esteem only what is established:
> Their minds
> Are little cells of ice.[25]

Teachers who refuse to be co-creators esteem only what they themselves establish, and they deny those they teach the role of co-creator.

The fourth element in the relation is the teacher and student (and content, too) as *sacraments* to one another. As sacraments, teacher and student image in their own ways the multitudinous variety and glory and grace of the universe, and the infinite variety of existence possibilities lying before them. Every weaver of fairy tales, every psychologist, every shaman, rabbi, and guru knows that if you pick up even one thread of reality and follow it to its end, it will take you to the heart of the universe. Standing in a relation of sacrament to each other, subjects offer the possibility of being this kind of thread.

REVELATION: WHAT IS IT TOWARD?

The final question of this chapter concerns the direction of revelation. If subject matter is embodied, enfleshed, and incarnated in such a way that the revelation of subject matter occurs, what happens next? What is its direction? Toward what end is such teaching directed?

Once again, Buber can help us. Buber tells us that in periods of culture that had a particular view of what it was to be human, in times when there was universal agreement or generally accepted standards, teachers could hold up a "figure" of universal validity and say, "Here is where you are going." Buber says that the "gentleman" was one such figure, the "Christian" another, the "citizen" a third. But what are we to do, and where are we going in a culture where all such figures are gone? "When all figures are shattered, when no figure is able any more to dominate and shape the present human material, what is there left to form? Nothing but the image of God."[26]

Revelation of subject matter is directed toward the formation of the divine image. Revelation contemplates it, stands back from it in discipline and respect, boldly attempts to create it, and sees it as a face in every face, a life in every life, a hope in every hope. If what has been said in this chapter has validity, we can never see this face in all its fullness. Indeed, every religious tradition is adamant in saying those who look full in the face of the divinity cannot continue to live.

Still, we do have glimpses of the lineaments of this mysterious image, and they already claim us in what we have read thus far. The following chapters are directed to tracing those lines, to giving some flesh to them, and to pronouncing their names. The names, of course, are not new and are already known, but they will be given place here as coordinates for the geography of teaching, symbols of its rightness, criteria for its truth. And what are their names? They are these: *The grace of power* leading to communion, and *re-creation* leading to justice and peace.

Teaching as the incarnation of subject matter that leads to the revelation of subject matter finds the subject revealed in the moment of ethical, moral, responsible choice, where the capacity to do or not do, to choose or not choose, to speak or not speak, lies before the subject (the person). In other words, if revelation happens, the subject receives the grace of power, discovering in the depths of the self capacities and abilities both to receive and to act from the subject's (person's) own subjectivity.

The discovered power is not yet fully human, however. Indeed, it is not true subjectivity if it is revealed as power of the subject alone. Thus, there is a second discovery. It is a discovery of power as power-with, of being as subject as being-with, of choosing existence possibilities in relation to being-in-existence-with, where, to use Gabriel Marcel's phrase, *"Esse est co-esse:* To be is to be with." The discovery of freedom that comes in facing the possibilities in existence is a higher freedom, the spirit's freedom, a freedom of religious tradition. It is a freedom that releases us from compulsive and competitive individualism and leads us to communion.

If revelation leads us to communion, especially communion with the other participating subjects of the world, then the moral demands of communion appear, and we discover yet another answer to the question of what revelation is directed to: namely, justice. Communion with others will necessarily move us to remove barriers, lessen whatever pain we can, and design modes of human being-together that acknowledge that all being has the ontological vocation to be subject; that not only are the humans revealed as subjects, but the world itself stands as subject to be accepted, to be reverenced, to be loved. Revelation will thus impel the work of justice, until all are one.

Finally, the vision of all as one is the vision of peace, of *shalom*, of reconciliation. The revelation of the *Imago Dei* is of a universal harmony, an Eden existence once again where "All that has divided us will merge; and then compassion will be wedded to power; and then women and men will be strong; and then all will share equally in the earth's abundance; and then all will be peacemakers in the places where each lives."[27]

This vision is central to understanding the following chapters on power and re-creation. Admittedly, power, communion, justice, and peace are profound subjects and not always offered as the fruit and end and direction of teaching. But this may turn out to be precisely what is wanting in teaching: We think in terms that are unworthy of us; we think too narrowly; we do not dare a vocation to the universe. But teaching *is* at best such a vocation, a calling to re-create a planet, all the stellar space surrounding it, and all the dreams and visions and hopes of the planet's inhabitants. The way of teaching offered in this book is the way of imagination—of religious imagination—where, having incarnated subject matter so that it leads to the revelation of subject matter, we discover that we (participating subjects) have received the grace of power in order to help re-create a world of communion, of justice, and of peace.

To the nature of this power, and to the dynamics residing within it, we will turn in chapter 5.

5. The Grace of Power

In a beautiful essay written some years ago for the *British Journal of Religious Education,* Edward Robinson makes an illuminating distinction. He writes of times in life when veils are suddenly removed or demands are made upon us or existence possibilities are set before us—what I have called revelation. Robinson says such experiences draw from us a kind of answering posture, *Seinbejahung,* a German word, "which quite untranslatably expresses the kind of positive response that is . . . the heart of religious experience. We are encountered by 'Sein'—life, existence, reality; it is up to us whether we respond to it with a 'ja' or a 'nein.' " Robinson suggests this is the capacity to say "yes" to our whole experience of what is real in life, as well as to our own potentialities—*Ichbejahung* or saying "yes" to ourselves.[1]

This capacity to say "yes," to say our own yes, not one we are told to say, and then to act on it symbolizes our readiness to receive the grace of power. As indicated in chapter 4, teaching as genuine revelation of subject matter moves to this when the other (learner) becomes able to make a choice, to initiate an action, to respond to a demand. Put more simply, the grace of power is present when we discover our own power and then exercise it, when we are enabled through revelation to act intelligently, humanly, responsibly, and religiously as beings in the world.[2]

In this chapter, I want both to examine the claiming of power as the outcome of teaching and to investigate the meaning of power. I will then move to a brief study of educational orientations that might assist empowerment, and finally to the major task of this chapter: to ask the question, "What is power for?"

In setting the above as the task of the chapter, I am aware that I am moving the focus from teacher to learner. In so doing, I have come to the moment of teaching described in chapter 2 as form-giving. Having taken part in engagement (the confrontation and interchange with subject matter), people begin to take hold of their own lives through integrating subject matter, thus giving their lives a unique, indelible, newly created and creative, unrepeatable form. But they also engage in the task of giving form to the world, consciously and responsibly and as a moral act. This chapter is based on the assumption that once we begin to give form not only to our own lives but to our world as well, we are exercising power publicly: We have become political.

UNDERSTANDINGS OF POWER

Power is a word that elicits many and varied emotional reactions. For some people, power is a dirty word. They feel we demean and soil ourselves by having anything to do with it. For a teacher to take such a stance seems to me disingenuous at best and scandalous at worst, for all teaching is an exercise of power. I suggest the emotional responses come not from power itself, but from the way it is understood and the way it is exercised. The questions this raises for us, then, are, "What do we understand by power?" and "What is involved in exercising and in teaching others to exercise power?"

Power is an ambiguous word. We see evidence of this in the way it is differently addressed by some of the world's best-known and most influential thinkers. Max Weber, for one, defines power as the possibility of forcing one's own will, whatever it may be, on the conduct of others. Hannah Arendt, by contrast, understands power as the capacity to agree in uncoerced communication on some community action.[3] Rollo May offers a typology that differentiates meanings by distinguishing five types of power: (1) exploitative power, which May identifies with force; (2) manipulative power, which is power over another; (3) competitive power, which is power against another; (4) nutritive power, which is power for another; and (5) integrative power, which is power with another.[4] In the first and second types, the other is not respected. In the last two types, the other is not only respected but cherished and loved as well. Talcott Parsons contributes to the discussion by naming four ways we exercise power: persuasion, activation of commitments, inducement, and coercion.[5] Elizabeth Janeway, drawing on the lives of oppressed peoples, examines what she calls the "powers of the weak," calling two of these powers essential: bonding and disbelief.[6]

Historically, religious traditions have had much to say about power, but what they say is characteristically paradoxical. Often, a great religious figure demonstrates power by exhibiting powerlessness: one thinks of Gandhi's *satyagraha* or soul force; of Francis of Assisi's divesting himself of all worldly goods, even his clothes; or of Jesus, who did not think being God a thing to be clung to, but instead "emptied himself" of power and became obedient to death, even to death on the cross.

Powerlessness, however, contains its own ambiguities. For one, those who have felt themselves without power have devised innumerable strategies for creating the illusion of power (or in an alternative reading, created forms of power different from the prevailing ones). Jean Johnson, schooled in Hindu wisdom, speaks of several ways to greet a neighbor which can be tactics of the powerless: sweet talk, force, bribery, dividing and conquering, creating an illusion, ignoring till you have decided on a method of handling, not getting in someone else's debt, and when all else fails, leaving a couple of mice.[7] But powerlessness possesses a still further complication. Powerlessness has often been praised as natural, acceptable, and even virtuous, notably in situations where the powerful are addressing the powerless: men to women, clergy to laity, adults to children, conquerors to conquered, and even teachers to students. When powerlessness is held up as a virtue, it might clarify the situation to look at who is holding it up for whom.

Having acknowledged all this, I want to propose that power is basically *capacity* and *ability*. As we have seen above, Weber calls power a possibility: Arendt calls it a capacity. Such is power's root meaning, its etymology. To refine the definition further, we can say that power is the capacity and ability to *act*, but we must immediately distinguish two fundamental elements within that definition. First, power is capacity and ability to act as *receiver*, in the sense of being receptive, attentive, and aware of the address of Being. Thus power is a capacity schooled by the contemplative and ascetic imaginations, with their attitudes of listening, watching, waiting, and seeing. But secondly, power is also capacity and ability to act as an *agent*, a doer, schooled by the creative and archetypal imaginations, with their attitudes of crafting, forming, making, and symbolizing. In the pages that follow, I will stress the latter aspect, returning to the power of receptivity at the end of this chapter and again in chapter 6.

The above definition of power draws on the knowledge that each human being has the vocation to be a subject who not only can act, but who has the responsibility to act in the world. All genuine teaching is implicitly directed to help learners come to this place of power. Reverend Jesse Jackson embodies this insight as he goes from school to school in the United States teaching young black people to acknowledge "I am SomeBody." And yet, for a great many people, the dawning knowledge of their capacities to act receptively or actively can be very frightening, especially if they have known only powerlessness. Such people are involved in the difficult task, to use Marge Piercy's phrase, of "unlearning to not speak." Such "unlearning" is, put positively, an impulse to personhood that can attract and repel at the same time. In her novel *Surfacing,* Margaret Atwood speaks of the letting go of dependency that is involved in acknowledging that one has power as well as of the risks involved in claiming power:

This above all, to refuse to be a victim. Unless I can do that, I can do nothing. I have to recant, give up the old belief that I am powerless and because of it nothing I can do will ever hurt anyone. A lie which was always more disastrous than the truth would have been. The word games, the winning and losing games are finished; at the moment there are no others but they will have to be invented, withdrawing is no longer possible and the alternative is death.[8]

Because taking responsibility for one's own power can be a frightening prospect, a teacher must be the learner's guarantor in such situations that accepting such power is the right thing to do. Indeed, the teacher must be a prod, even a midwife, enabling the other—and the other's gifts—to come to birth.

Contemporary theological thought gives a further nuance to such empowering in teaching as a religious activity. Theology does this by addressing the tendency to separate religion from people's tasks in the world, a recurring phenomenon among many so-called religious people. Even though many religious teachers have taught and demonstrated with their lives how irrevocably bound are one's religious and social convictions—we think of Dorothy Day, of Dom Helder Camera of Brazil, or of Dietrich Bonhoeffer—the fact remains that many people consider religion a private affair. The emergence of liberation theologies, of theology "from below" (which is from the perspective of the poor), and especially of political theology is changing this privatized notion dramatically. Indeed, it is the nature of political theology, says its foremost exponent, Johannes Baptist Metz, to be first of all "a critical correction of present-day theology inasmuch as this theology shows an extreme privatizing tendency, a tendency, that is, to center upon the private person rather than public, political society."[9] Imagined religiously, then, the power of which I speak, since it is a shared power, is directed toward creating a communion of intersubjectivity, a power of community where one's capacity and ability to act is with and for others as well as with and for oneself. It is the receptive power of saying "yes" to all of Being, to all beings. A teacher working with such a vision of power is a kind of priest, ordaining the learner into a world of responsibility. Addressed by such a vision, learners know the moment of ordination in response, and feel themselves close to playwright Ntozake Shange's "Lady in Purple," who expresses such empowering as: "A layin' on of hands; the holiness of myself released."[10] This is the grace of power: recognizing the holiness in ourselves released and sent forth, into the universe.

EDUCATIONAL ORIENTATIONS

If the teacher's work is geared toward mediating the grace of power, what will be the culture—the *cultura*—in which seeds for empowerment will grow? What will constitute the nutritive power of Rollo May's typology? Traditionally, the *cultura* in which growth occurs is called curriculum, the environment and materials designed to promote valued educational activity.[11] Therefore, before considering the question, "Power for what?" let us examine the kind of educational environments needed to foster power.

In *The Educational Imagination,* Elliot Eisner names five orientations we can adopt toward curriculum; each produces a somewhat different result.[12] Like all creditable schoolteachers, Elliot Eisner knows that the setting in which questions are posed in large part determines the answers that are possible:

the dominant framework for viewing curriculum has consequences for the practical operation of schools; each orientation harbors an implicit conception of educational virtue. Furthermore, each orientation serves both to legitimize certain educational practices and to negatively sanction others. It also functions as an ideological center around which political support can be gathered.[13]

These are the five basic orientations identified by Eisner and his colleague Elizabeth Vallance:

1. The development of cognitive processes, where the mind is conceived as a collection of faculties and aptitudes and the curriculum is designed to enhance the ability to infer, to speculate, to locate and solve problems, to remember, to visualize, to extrapolate, and so on.
2. Academic rationalism, which concentrates on those subject matters most worthy of study, the liberal arts, the "best" of human history, as in a Great Books approach or in the quadrivium and trivium of classical education—the knowledge of history and traditions.
3. Personal relevance, where the educational development of the individual is given primacy and attention is directed not only to what he or she chooses, but to what he or she finds meaningful.
4. Curriculum as technology, which emphasizes knowing *how,* where a means-ends rationality is the basis, and where measurable goals and objectives are offered to help learners design and carry out effective and efficient plans.
5. Social adaptation/social reconstruction, where the former derives its aims and content from an analysis of the society around it, and is designed to help learners "fit in" to society; whereas reconstruction's goal is to produce a critical consciousness to help alleviate the ills of society and to transform it.[14]

Over the years, I have worked with all of these orientations, introducing students to their differences, and helping students see how each orientation leads to distinct but related conclusions. Together we discovered that if certain shifts are made, and if we can see these orientations as *complementary* rather than *conflicting*, we can effect a somewhat different and much wider ground for teaching. Our approach has been to posit one of the orientations as broad enough to encompass the others, indeed as *needing* the others. Our choice among the orientations, based on principles to be articulated below, is that of the social. I propose, however, one major change in that orientation: its name. I prefer not to speak of *social reconstruction,* a phrase with a long history and specific meaning in educational circles, and thus open to misinterpretation or too-quick understanding. Instead, the orientation is better named *social re-creation,* with emphasis placed equally on each term in the phrase. *Social* is stressed to overcome the competitive and individualistic; to point to the necessary political dimension of teaching. *Re-creation* is stressed to overcome the technical and rationalistic connotations of "construct" and to point to the necessary religious and artistic dimensions of teaching.

The argument for this choice and change is threefold. First, the widest possible arena is needed to teach in the direction of mediating the grace of power. If our basic orientation is the social vocation to create a more just public world—a vocation to be exercised not only in one's own country, but in the global village—then the other four orientations do not become competitors, they become companions. For in order to re-create, one needs the development of cognitive processes, namely, literacy. Although literacy depends on the abilities to infer, to extrapolate, to speculate, and to visualize, it does not end with the acquisition of those abilities. Instead, literacy must become the capacity to read the signs of one's culture and environment, a capacity that enables looking to become seeing, seeing to become believing, and learning to become revelation. "Acquiring literacy does not involve memorizing sentences, words, or syllables—lifeless objects unconnected to an existential universe—but rather an attitude of creation and re-creation, a self-transformation producing a stance of intervention in one's context."[15]

We will also need academic rationalism in our vision. That is, we must draw on the wisdom of the past, on the "best" that has been produced. But in a still-to-be-created social order, that orientation demands that the wisdom of all peoples of all nations be included—and not only the wisdom garnered from those with access to print, preaching, or other forms of publication. We will also need the motivation and impetus of learning for personal relevance as a curricular orientation, in order to bring the fullness of each person, each individual "I" to birth. Finally, an orientation to social re-creation needs the best of technical genius, all the while pointing beyond the technique of material innovation to the making of human wholeness.

The second point in the argument for incorporating the first four orientations under the wider umbrella of the last is that such incorporation allows education to be understood as an engagement with persons of every age, and not just with children. If one reads Eisner carefully, the arguments made for one or the other of the orientations seem to be based on the assumption that one is designing curriculum for children or for schools. But if education is lifelong, as common wisdom assumes and as practical wisdom appreciates, then even after the basic processes and technologies are learned and the wisdom of the past is integrated, something compels us throughout all our lives to go beyond what we have already realized. To facilitate this, the best of the orientations is the social one, for it entices the learner to continue to go beyond what has thus far been accomplished, while discovering the grace of power in every area, through all five orientations in concert.

The third point in the argument for reorienting the orientations is one persistently and patiently made in all of Gabriel Moran's educational philosophy: Education is not equal to schooling, and, Moran's more recent and correlative point, teaching is not equal to school teaching.[16] One of the problems associated with *conflicting* conceptions of curriculum—that is, one of the things that causes them to *be* in conflict—is the implicit assumption that the school is the only educator. If one adopts this view, one is almost forced to choose one curricular orientation over another, because no one institution can do everything. But if one adopts Moran's view, education is seen as: the *end* (end both as direction and end as completion) of the interplay of several *forms* of learning; what *results* when community, leisure, work, and conceptual thought are in interaction, and not just the result of the conceptualization element alone; and as the *interchange* between, for example, schooling, family, job, and retreat. Education is not equal to schooling alone; it is far broader.

Thus, no *one* orientation will be enough.[17] Necessarily, education will be at its best in an educational environment created from the assumption that not only is the entire world revelatory of meaning, but that the entire world is educational as well. Such a vision empowers the teaching vocation of all persons, and not only the schoolteacher. This realization illuminates the presence of the teaching that continually goes on in the churches, in the family setting, among friends, at work, during concerts and baseball games, and in the still, quiet moments when a child contemplates a daisy, allowing the daisy to teach all it knows of earth and sun and sky.

POWER FOR WHAT?

In choosing the educational orientation of social re-creation, I have already begun responding to the questions, "What is the grace of power for—toward what end?" and "Why exercise power?" These are teleological questions, and they depend on the articulation of a philosophical position to support a response. I turn now to the articulation of that position.

In her poem "Living in the Third World," Constance Urdang writes,

> A beggar crouches in his own filth,
> Displaying stumps of fingers, running sores;
> He says the egg of the world is cracked,
> And from its wounds
> Poisoned tears fall, like rain over Jakarta[18]

There is a terrible urgency in the world we live in. From the wounds of the planet, terror, tears, and blood flow like a river—

not only, as the beggar says, in Jakarta, but in Mexico City and Addis Ababa, in Belfast and Beirut, and (less obviously) in Columbus and Chicago, in London, Paris, and New York. We need educational wisdom to reclaim and renew the words, "peace and hope and new life, *too*, are flowing." For we are at a time in the history of the planet where the primary issue for religious people, indeed for all people, is not redemption of the soul, but redemption of the world (Monika Hellwig).

The appeal to wisdom for the world is an appeal to philosophy, but of a particular kind; it is an appeal to *political philosophy*. By definition, philosophers are lovers of wisdom. But where the speculative philosopher must necessarily stand back and reflect, at least for a while, the political philosopher is a philosopher in action, loving wisdom in the doing, the incarnating, the embodying. The political philosopher does not only think about and talk about action. The political philosopher takes principle and conviction and dwells in them, gives them flesh. Involved as we teachers are in the incarnation of subject matter in a public domain, and therefore in the task of embodying our beliefs through quite specific action in the world, we find ourselves in the role of political philosophers. Or, to put it another way— the boldest way possible—*every teacher has a political vocation.*[19]

The term *political* here refers to an incarnated symbolic form: the way we humans choose to exercise and share—or not share— power among ourselves in the public setting. The political forms we create are the shapes and structures we make for negotiating and interchanging power, for mediating the grace of power to others. Usually, we apply the term political to that *polis* or social system which is outside the sphere of our immediate activity, whether that is family or school, church or job site. But *every* human grouping is a political system, a body politic. Therefore, to say that the teacher has a political vocation is in one sense simply to name what *is*. However, I will be far more specific and direct than that.

In his educational writing, Dwayne Huebner fleshes out the teacher's political vocation by suggesting that schoolteachers and administrators "talk about the political tasks of making a more just public world. Talk about it in such a way that the political and economic nature of education can be clearly seen."[20] He

proposes three rights as ingredients of this task: (1) the uncon-
ditional respect for the political, civil, and legal rights of students as free people participating in a public world; (2) the right
of access to the wealth in the public domain, which is primarily
the knowledge, traditions, and skills that shape and increase a
person's power in the public world; (3) the right of every individual, regardless of age, to participate in the shaping and
reshaping of the institutions within which he or she lives.[21]

To my mind, what Huebner is taking pains to describe is the
vocation to mediate power. Huebner's contribution is naming
the specifics of that vocation. When addressed and incorporated
into educational planning, those specifics enable the people we
teach to claim the power that is theirs, not only in order to
participate in the world, but in order to shape it and reshape
it. We instruct others in order to help develop their cognitive
processes, but the question that remains is, "For what?" We
hand on the traditions, the lore, the history of the race, but the
question that remains is, "For what?" We try to develop the
sense of being people, the capacity for critical consciousness, of
course; but the question that remains is, "For what?" We engage
in the exploration of technology, but the question that remains
is, "For what?" I use the companion word "vocation" when
speaking of teaching, to appeal to the religious grounding of
the work and to point out that the political vocation is not only
directed toward enabling the presence of certain capacities, but
directed toward the *use* of those capacities in service to others:
healing, creating, and re-creating. My powers are not only for
me. I possess them not only to say "yes" to myself. To be is to-
be-with; thus my powers are for the universe and for all its
inhabitants. If I am to be a complete human being, no other
vocation is worthy of me. Thus, I answer the question "For
what?" or "What is the grace of power toward?" quite simply.
The grace of power is directed toward the re-creation of the
world. Teaching, when seen as an activity of religious imagination, is an act of incarnating subject matter in ways which (or
in order to) reveal subject matter so that subjects, in communion with each other, are able to exercise power: the capacity and
ability to act receptively, intelligently, humanly, responsibly, and
religiously in transforming the universe.

THE POWERS TO CLAIM

If we grant that such is the appropriate and necessary direction of teaching today, we can specify with more clarity those powers most important to claim as we undertake the teaching task. I believe there are five such powers: (1) the power to receive; (2) the power to rebel; (3) the power to resist; (4) the power to reform; (5) the power to love.

THE POWER TO RECEIVE

Charles Peguy, the French essayist and poet, is reported to have said that everything begins in mysticism and ends in politics. The impetus to act in the public realm is best grounded when it arises out of the quiet and reflection of the mystical sense, where we apprehend the connections, the visible and invisible ties, binding all creation. This apprehension is fostered by cultivating receptivity, listening, waiting-on—not in the sense of subservience, but in order to hear the voice of creation. If we want to see *and* hear the cracking egg of the world—from

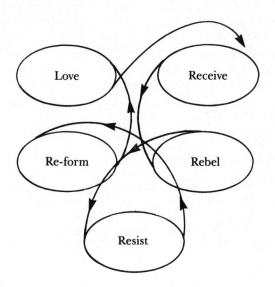

which the poisoned tears fall—the first power we need is receptivity, the willingness to be still so as to be attentive. Hurried, unreflective activity is frenzied, unproductive. In contrast, acting that proceeds from receptivity has at least the possibility of a strong and nurtured beginning.

In a world of rampant hunger, poverty, and homelessness, such receptivity will help us be more aware of the planet's situation. If the power to receive what is there is cultivated, then a second power becomes necessary, a power rooted in the prophetic stance of facing the given situation and saying, "no."

THE POWER TO REBEL

Why claim the power to rebel for those we teach? Why rebel? Because of the situation. And what is the situation? The possibility of Holocaust. Anne Frank is dead; six million are dead. We live in a post-Holocaust world, wounded and scarred for all time by that fissure of evil. Even though the Holocaust is not always the content of our teaching or our educational work, the power we enable needs to be shaped and formed by this wound in the body politic, *so that nothing like it will ever happen again.* Swastikas are being painted in our world once more. The political vocation empowers the capacity to rebel against this kind of evil, this kind of terror, this kind of sin.

Why rebel? Once again, because of the possibility of future Holocaust, not only of another Hiroshima or Nagasaki, but of a burning which would dwarf them all. In *Lightning East and West,* James Douglass paints the situation through a brief yet power-filled catechesis:

Q. *What is Trident?*
A. Trident is the end of the world.
Q. *What do you mean?*
A. Trident is a nuclear submarine being built now which will be able to destroy 408 cities or areas at one time, each with a blast five times more powerful than the Hiroshima bomb. Trident is 2040 Hiroshimas. One Trident submarine can destroy any country on earth. A fleet of Trident submarines (30 are planned) can end life on earth.
Q. *I don't understand.*
A. Good, we're getting somewhere. What is it you don't understand?

Q. *A submarine that equals 2040 Hiroshimas. How can anyone understand?*
A. Begin with a meditation. To understand Trident, say the word "Hiroshima." Reflect on its meaning for one second. Say and understand "Hiroshima" again. And again. And again. 2040 times.[22]

Why rebel? Because of the situation. We cannot do our educational work in a vacuum; the curriculum, the environment in which we educate, is a world. And that world, in political terms, is not "theirs," in contrast to "ours": It is the only world all of us have. John Fry's proposal to theologians is also pertinent to teachers. "I propose," he writes, "that theologians write theology from the standpoint of the mother in Bombay (or Pittsburgh) whose child has just starved to death. She would not be theology's primary reader, and her situation would not provide theology's subject matter. But her rage and grief would provide its angle of vision."[23] Similarly, I propose that teachers teach in this light, where the rage and grief of the world's suffering provide our angle of vision, too.

To claim the power to rebel is to hold such pictures in mind as we teach, so that suffering is not seen as the "other's" in contrast to our own. Perhaps the most articulate advocate of rebellion, Albert Camus, reflects that:

from the moment that a movement of rebellion begins, suffering is seen as a collective experience—as the experience of everyone. Therefore the first step for a mind overwhelmed by the strangeness of things is to realize that this feeling of strangeness is shared with all men and women and that the entire human race suffers from the division between itself and the rest of the world. The unhappiness experienced by a single man or woman becomes collective unhappiness. In our daily trials, rebellion plays the same role as does the "cogito" in the category of thought: it is the first clue. But this clue lures the individual from his or her solitude. Rebellion is the common ground on which every human being bases his or her first values. *I rebel—therefore we exist.*[24]

Camus's citation of the word *cogito* is a reminder of how abstract much teaching has become; at home in the world of *cogito* or of *cogito ergo sum*; less at home in the world of "I rebel, and therefore we exist;" at home in a world of *ego sum*, less at home in an entire communion of subjectivity inclusive of the entire human race. Nonetheless, I am not the first educator to propose the power to rebel. Paulo Freire, in another context, speaks of its educational impact: "I consider that attitude of rebellion as one of the most promising aspects of our political life—not because I espoused it as a form of action, but because it represented a symptom of advancement, an introduction to a more complete humanity."[25]

Rebellion, finally, is the expression of feeling that comes in the naming of those particular destructive evils and suffering that are not to be tolerated. It is never rebellion for the sake of rebellion. Engaging in rebellion means claiming the right to say that evil, divisiveness, and inhumanity are wrong; and, by doing so, affirming and keeping alive the human feeling in the protest. And when feeling is alive, hope is present. Once such feeling is expressed, however, a third claim to power—and power to claim—appears.

THE POWER TO RESIST

In contrast to rebellion, which is attitudinal and rooted in feeling, resistance is work against, active opposition, withstanding. Resistance is refusal to accept the way things are because things could be different. When active resistance occurs and those who are oppressed legitimately rise against the oppressor, it is the former who are usually labeled "violent," "barbaric," or "inhuman." Oppressors never seem able to see themselves as violent.[26] And so a first quality of resistance is to being defined by others.

The power to resist begins in the youngest human beings as they say their "no's" in early childhood. They say them over against, because they are trying to understand who they are as selves. But their first "no" is made legitimate or illegitimate generally, by the kind of authority and adult power they face. If it is genuine, it will not be coercive authority, nor an authority put on and off like a cloak—assumed. Rather it will be demonstrated by a truth and sincerity offered in response to the young person's resistance. Great teachers, whether in schools or elsewhere, listen to the "no" of resistance and explore the reasons why it is said.

Throughout life, we are continually faced with the choice of exercising the power to resist. Often we assign it to the realm of those striving to overcome governmental power that they deem unjust, people with names like "partisan" or "guerilla" or "freedom fighter." But when our own political vocations are recognized and the re-creation of the world is accepted as an educational issue, what does resistance mean? To what in the teaching/learning situation must "no" be said? Specific answers are hard to come by, but we can find four basic areas in which resistance is needed.

First, we must resist privatizing, ghettoizing, and domesticating the teaching act. To domesticate an animal is to tame it and thus render it harmless. Used metaphorically, domestication is the process whereby groups in power seek to channel or neutralize the potentially resistant forces let loose when people realize they are exploited.[27] Domestication keeps people from thinking of themselves as subjects; privatizing and ghettoizing keep people from thinking of the world as subject.

Second, we must resist *any* abrogation of legal, civil, and political rights. Parents of minor children and schoolteachers of children and adolescents often must work out many forms of negotiating power whenever the human rights of the younger (less so the older, but not always) are being violated. Tragically, young people often have no sense of their rights. Rather than grudgingly "permit" students their rights, teachers can exemplify resistance by teaching them their rights, and by urging understanding of basic human rights in the civic context.[28]

In the United States, on December 5, 1955, the newly appointed head of the Montgomery Improvement Association stood in a church pulpit and issued a cry for resistance, claiming the future as the power energizing his cry:

If we protest courageously, and yet with dignity and Christian love, when the history books are written in the future, somebody will have to say, "There lived a race of people, of black people, of people who had the moral courage to stand up for their rights. And thereby they injected a new meaning into the veins of history and civilization."[29]

This passage is in the best tradition of resistance, and one all educators might copy.

Third, we must resist unequal allocation of the wealth in the public domain, especially the knowledge, traditions, and skills that increase a person's power in the public world. This can mean working to create better institutions, or it can mean sharing one's own gifts. But in the overabundance of the Western democracies, in light of the starvation of the majority of the world's peoples, it could mean resistance to the standards of living assumed in the overabundant society and the gradual but continuing activity of dispossession, relinquishment, and letting go—the exercise of our ascetic imaginations.

Finally, we must resist taking or espousing any position that excludes people from shaping the institutions in which they live. In this regard, the educator needs to resist the tendency to be too independent, on the one hand—*not* sharing power, not necessarily out of malice but because it is easier to do things oneself—and the tendency to accept the dependency of others who are still unwilling to exercise their own power, on the other. The ideal to be espoused is *inter*dependence.

THE POWER TO REFORM

In Roman Catholic ecclesiastical tradition, the church is spoken of as *ecclesia semper reformanda*. The translation is interesting: "the church always in the process of being reformed," that is, an institution whose final form is never fixed, whose form must be shaped and reshaped in order for it to be appropriate to its particular place and time.

Thus when I speak about the need to claim the power to reform as part of educational activity, I am saying that reforming is a given in life. If an organism is living and dynamic, a pattern of forming and reforming soon establishes itself. The continuing re-creation of form signals an organism's health, for a living organism is always taking in material not of its own system, splitting it up, and reforming it into living matter. Reforming becomes a political act when it is directed to the content and material constituting the body politic itself, that is, toward the institution or organization in which we find ourselves working.

As with resistance, the political vocation of reformation may be seen as belonging only to those who have been granted authority in the institution or organization. Or—and this is what I am arguing for—it can be understood as essential to the vocation of all, and thus a reason why mediating the grace of power is a critical component of all genuine teaching. We have already seen examples of reforming in the teaching act in chapter 3: verbal, earth, embodied, and discovered forms. We have seen it in chapter 4 as well, where indirect communication is directed toward the learner reforming the sense of self, akin to the psalmist's call: "Create a clean heart in me, O Lord, and renew a right spirit within me" (Psalm 52:12). Here I am trying to extend that reforming work to the institutional level and on political grounds. For, "just as scientific revolutions are inaugurated by a growing sense that the existing paradigm no longer functions adequately, political revolutions are inaugurated by a growing sense that the existing institutions have ceased adequately to meet the problems posed by an environment that they have in part created."[30] Today, that growing sense of the inadequacy of human forms is perhaps the most significant political current of our time. When learners lay claim to the power of reform, they are searching to create a world order in which freely chosen, interdependent, and mutual exchange is no longer hindered by narrow, authoritarian, dominating patterns. An educational form which does not view the world as its curricular environment is simply too limited a view for our times.

THE POWER TO LOVE

The idea that "everything begins in mysticism and ends in politics" is incomplete. We must also say, "and the purpose of politics, of course, is to return us once again to mysticism." And I would add that the political vocation of mediating the grace of power is incomplete if it does not end in love. Mysticism is the setting, yes; but it is not enough simply to be convinced intellectually or personally of the oneness (the relatedness) of all beings. A dynamic pulses within mysticism itself, pushing beyond to a caring for, a wishing well, a seeking after the happiness of the other.

I am not suggesting that love is always absent from the political vocation. Both Gandhi and Martin Luther King, Jr. knew its power and taught it not only to their followers, but to the rest of the world. Indeed, it was King who taught that deeds of love make God credible. A thought based on the poet W. H.

6. Re-Creation

The implicit, and often explicit, assumption in chapter 5 is the necessity to create a new educational environment in today's world, a geography of and for curriculum that takes into account an interdependent world characterized by a communion of interdependent subjects. The burden of this chapter will be to offer an answer to the question, "How might this be done?" I will address the issue of the nature of teaching as transformative and re-creative activity, designed in such a way that teachers do not become involved in ghettoizing or domesticating their own lives and the lives of those they teach. Chapter 5 was more proscriptive and prescriptive about this work, but this chapter will be descriptive. It will propose, as did chapter 2, a teaching paradigm. Here, however, the paradigm is directed not only to the individual teacher acting on her or his own, but to the entire community as an agent of teaching; not toward the forming of subject matter, but to the reforming of the setting in which subject matter is incarnated.

POINTS OF DEPARTURE

The paradigm's description will begin with the experience of being "strange" or an outsider. When completed, the paradigm will be a form of *paideia*, that is, an entire curricular environment or culture that educates by being a special setting, whole in itself. This paradigm draws on the notion of generative themes. Paulo Freire has taught us that generative themes exist in culture, contain their own opposites, and suggest educational tasks.[1] For our purposes, however, although I will focus on generative themes, I will not do so in order to attend to their opposites, but to explore the originative and life-giving connotation of the term *generative* itself. I will name five themes in the re-creation paradigm: silence, awareness, mourning, bonding, and birth;

each of which bears the one that follows it. Along with each theme I will also suggest a particular teaching and curricular task to which the theme impels us. Before moving to this paradigm, however, I wish to lay a foundation by stating two points of departure. The first is personal, although not entirely so (the personal is always political); the other is educational.

THE OUTSIDER AS POINT OF DEPARTURE

Several years ago, as a participant in a workshop on authority and power in institutions, I was asked to describe myself in terms of the place where I worked and to say what it was I "carried" for that place. I thought for a moment and then talked of myself as faculty member. Of a faculty of eighteen, six were United Church of Christ, six were American Baptist, six were other. I was one of the "others." Of the six others, five were Protestant, one was Roman Catholic. I was the Catholic. Sixteen were ordained, two were not. I was one of the two. Sixteen were married, two were not. I was one of the two. Seventeen were teachers of theology; one was in the field of religious education. I was that one. Sixteen were men; two were women. I am a woman.

At that point in the exercise, the woman leading my small group said to me gently, "Maria, it might be interesting for you sometime to examine why it is you continually place yourself in the position of an outsider." Being somewhat defensive, I replied instantly (although admittedly, to myself), "I'm *not* an outsider."

Yet I found the question profound and provocative, and it stayed with me. My first response was to say I was involved in completion: that my work as an unordained person, as a religious educator, as a Catholic, was to offer the presence of what was under-represented, or unrepresented in the curriculum. But upon reflection, I realized that the metaphor of completion kept me as outsider, that completion connoted a fullness to content already there. Rather than being reformed, it needed only something additional. My second response was to move to the metaphor of reconciliation, seeing my work in religious education as healing the divisions in theology; seeing the work of a Catholic as healing a religious split; seeing my woman-presence as a move toward overcoming the division between women and men. That was somewhat closer to the truth, but still did not capture the essence of my experience.

And then I read Catherina Halkes, the Dutch theologian, writing on feminist theology. She was discussing conditions necessary for dialogue, where "the first is an attitude of openness, of being ready to listen with real interest, to put one's own theological 'position' aside, to be receptive and able to reason things out with others and for the moment, not to force arguments to prove oneself right and in any case not to prejudge the other side."[2] She concluded by speaking eloquently for the necessity of this condition, saying openness was needed not only in order to start with the right attitude but also for the content of the dialogue. The reason she gave was that the dialogue feminist theology is looking for "*contains the 'strange,' the 'unusual,' the 'unaccustomed' as an inherent part of its content as well as a principle of interpretation.*"[3] In other words, if we want to open up and discover meaning, the hermeneutic principle is not what is obvious, but what is strange and surprising; what is outside, the outsider. It is the thing that does not "fit" which lures us and leads us on.

My own reaction to Halkes's passage was a moment of true revelation. For in reading the word *strange*, I realized that what I had been alluding to in my own experience as an outsider was a kind of knowing available in no other way than by being an outsider. It was a knowing to be revered and deepened, rather than discarded. But beyond that, I recognized that I had stumbled upon an almost universal human experience: that of being an outsider. The standpoint of outsider gives a view that does not correspond to the old maps, the normal and familiar way of viewing human experience. From their long sojourn in the country of the strange, outsiders know an uncharted territory of human existence. Outsiders bring an entirely different angle of vision to the whole human enterprise. Outsiders provoke re-creation.

THE THREE CURRICULA AS POINT OF DEPARTURE

Before moving on to the paradigm for creating a curricular environment that establishes a new geography for education, a second point of departure merits attention and examination.

This point is the three curricula all institutions teach—the explicit, the implicit, and the null. These curricula, brilliantly and originally illuminated by Elliot Eisner, are essential to the work of re-creation.[4] In Eisner's formulation, all institutions and all people teach these three curricula. The *explicit* curriculum is the actual courses of study, ideas, activities, stated plans, and procedures that are consciously presented and engaged in by teachers and by institutions. The explicit is what gets said, what gets offered, what gets attention, what gets printed.

The *implicit* curriculum, in contrast, is what gets said in what is suggested, what is "taught" by such things as organizational structure, forms of direct address (for example, the use of titles in contrast to first names), and patterns of decision making. The implicit curriculum refers not only to who speaks and who has access to the organs and forms of communication, but also to who gets heard, to whose ideas are built upon in what can be understood as the politics of talking (of communication and exchange). The implicit curriculum is what a school, an institution, or a person teaches by the *kind* of a place or person it is. Eisner quotes the Chinese painter Li-li Weng in distinguishing explicit and implicit: "First you see the hills in the painting; then you see the painting in the hills."[5]

The *null* curriculum, ironically and paradoxically, is a curriculum that exists because it does *not* exist. We include it, however, because ignorance is never neutral. Not being educated in something skews and biases the options that lie before us, the perspectives from which we see, the alternatives from which we might choose. Thus, we must pay attention to the null curriculum: to the areas of study left out; to all the unheard voices; to the many processes and procedures that remain untrod as paths toward learning, knowing, and understanding.

The existence of, indeed the genesis for, the paradigm I am about to present comes from the intersection of the "outsider" with the three curricula. Of the personal outsider experiences I named above, one is undoubtedly more "outside" than any of the others: that of being a woman in a man's world, that of learning there is indeed man's world and woman's place in it. But the revelation of the experience of women has led me to recognize a more general and universal situation and to discover its paradigm, one that is extraordinarily pregnant for the redesign, transformation, and re-creation of all education, for the geography of the teacher in today's world. I move now to a description of that paradigm, as a series of five steps or moments to contemplate, to engage, and to form, so that a new and more broadly representative environment for teaching might emerge and be released into the world.

SILENCE

As an initial step, when I examine the explicit, the implicit, and the null curricula from the perspective of being a woman, I discover immediately a silence about women, by women, and toward women. Often it is a deafening silence. The language excludes me. The bibliographical citations include me only sparingly if at all. My experiences and those of women throughout history tend not to be mentioned; or, if mentioned, they are limited to those women who were rulers or wives of "important" men. I am not surprised that women who do have access to public speech, to means of communication, to publication, entitle their works the way they do: for example, Tillie Olsen's "Silences," Adrienne Rich's "On Lies, Secrets and Silences," Rita Gross and Nancy Falk's description of the religious lives of

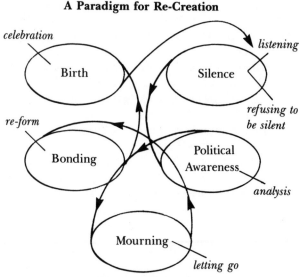

A Paradigm for Re-Creation

the themes and the tasks

773/7

ɔmen, "Unspoken Worlds," Carol Gilligan's "In a Different
Voice."[6] We women find ourselves surrounded by silences. And
if we do speak, we find the assumption persists that we women
speak more than men do, despite the fact that every major study
thus far published on the question reveals either that the opposite is true, or that men and women speak equally. I find the
clearest interpretation of *that* situation in the assumption that
women speak more than men because we are measured not
alongside males as speakers but against females as silent.

With reference to the null curriculum, or what is not taught,
an insight of critical importance comes from a 1960 work of
Valerie Saiving. She was studying the theology of sin in the work
of Reinhold Niebuhr and Anders Nygren, but at the same time
was reflecting on Margaret Mead and on her own experience.
Finding sin defined as "pride" and "self-love" and "will to power,"
Saiving questioned whether this definition adequately described
her own and other women's experience of sin, or whether her
own sinfulness was not better described by such issues as trivi-
ality, distractibility, diffuseness, dependence on others for self-
definition, refusal to name oneself.[7] I believe that Saiving's
insight is critically important because it raises two issues for
curriculum and teaching: (1) On whose experience do we draw
for our understandings of what it is to be human? (2) From
where do we draw the meanings and the definitions of all our
most central human questions, not only sin, but faith, death,
hope, love, intimacy, war, and peace?

This is only the beginning, however. For woman as outsider is
a metaphor, albeit a partial one, for an entire world of outsiders.
The woman I speak of is myself, a white, middle-class woman.
The silence of women of color is certainly more deafening, as
is the silence in historical and religious circles of the evils per-
petrated against women solely because of our sex. From Hindu
suttee, to Chinese footbinding, to African genital mutilation, to
European witch-burning, to the gynecological practice in the
United States of unnecessarily removing wombs and breasts,
our curricular emphases have tended to exclude contemplating
these "terrible things" as subjects of study.[8]

If we recognize woman as outsider, we discover a dynamism
within that recognition that leads us both to discover other

silent people and to hear other silences around us, silences
of those who are silent for reasons other than their gender.
(Nevertheless, we must not forget that throughout the world,
the poorest of the poor are, in fact, women and girls.) These
other people, female and male, are the outsiders because of
race, class, political conviction, economic position, religion, age,
or illiteracy. To all these silences, the teacher must give heed.
We even notice silences apparent in the powerful of the planet,
the quiet places in powerful men that have had to be destroyed
or forgotten if those men were to achieve the dubious competitive success held out to them as life's ideal. However, the silence
of the powerful is usually not the first silence to be entertained.

In teaching, the discovery of silence is not addressed initially
by rushing to include a wider representation of humanity, although such inclusion is, of course, needed. The too-quick inclusion of courses in women's studies, in black studies, in Asian
studies can implicitly convey that these are added-on, remedial,
compensatory, and not part of the mainstream. They can be
discarded as soon as funds dry up. Rather, the exploration of
silence and the silenced teaches us to realize that virtually all
teaching is conditioned and shaped and limited by the social
location and cultural conditioning of those who "create" knowledge. Thus the issue is not simply one of bringing additional perspectives into teaching and curriculum as a way of picking up
dropped stitches. Rather, what is at issue is the study of how our
approach to learning is formed by our sociocultural "location."[9]

Given this insight, the generative theme of silence implies a
twofold educational *task*. Out of the discovery of silence—indeed, of the culture of silence in which millions exist—this
generative theme impels us to take up the dual task of *listening*
to the silences around us and *refusing* to be silent any longer.

Listening and Refusing to Be Silent

Listening as a consciously chosen task enables us to hear and
to realize that curriculum is silent not only about women, but
about most of the world's peoples—women, men, and children—who are without political power. A letter smuggled from
a Philippine prison before the fall of Marcos says simply: "If
you want to hear what we are saying, listen *closely* to what we

are not allowed to say."[10] But we must also listen to the *actions* of the silenced. Judith Dorney comments that the silent are not being silent as their main work, and she challenges us to discover the answer to the question, "What are the silent doing?"[11] Attending to that question, in a variety of "silent" situations, we find the answer is almost always the same: The silent are carrying out the human work that keeps the world going. The silent cook the world's meals, dry the world's tears, heal the world's cuts and bruises, make the world's beds—for those who have them—clean the world's clothes and dishes, and wipe the world's noses. If this is true, the educational task of listening is primarily important for those who do most of the speechifying in the world. Thus, in the educational context, listening is especially incumbent on the teacher, allied as it is to the moment of contemplation. As with all silent work, listening has moments of sound within its texture. Nonetheless, listening is more attentive and tending than it is active and outgoing.

The companion to the listening task, refusing to be silent any longer, is especially incumbent on those who do much of the accepting of orders in the world. In the educational context, refusing to be silent is the task of the student, the learner. This task takes shape in finding one's own voice, the voices of others, and the voices of entire peoples. Mysteriously, listening and refusing to be silent is a form of obedience, if that word be understood to mean *ab audire*, to have one's hearing against the earth. As such, obedience calls up an image of the divinity suggested by Nelle Morton: God the Great Ear, who listens to the heart and sound of the universe.[12] The dual task of listening and refusing to be silent not only chastens the more negative meaning of silence as an evil to be eradicated, but also urges us to claim the positive aspect of silence as a holiness to be entered. Finally, if the task is taken on, a new generative theme is born, which, in turn, furthers the work of teaching. For silence gives birth to awareness.

AWARENESS—POLITICAL AWARENESS

Awareness. What does it mean? In a brief but beautiful essay, Martin Buber answers this question with insight.[13] He tells us there are three ways possible to enter any situation. The first is to go in with a list of conditions, qualities, circumstances we are looking for, perhaps even checking our list to see if they are present or absent. This is the way of observation. The second is almost the opposite. We bring no list. Instead, we trust our minds and hearts to pick up what is present in the situation, to see what is there, to await what is presented. This is the way of the onlooker. Buber tells us these two have a similar orientation in that the person entering the situation is an actor or agent in each: What is viewed is an object at some distance from the observer or the onlooker. Thus neither way of entering a situation "inflicts destiny" upon the person. But Buber offers a third possible way of entering the situation. If I choose that way, something entirely different occurs.

In a reflective moment of my life, I may enter a situation and find I am neither observer nor onlooker. Instead, I am met with the existence possibility where something addresses *me*, something says something to *me*, and I have to *do* with it. I may have to make a choice several years from now; I may immediately have to give all my goods to the poor; I may have to transform my life. I do not know exactly what I am to do. But what I do know is that in such a reflective moment, a word demanding an answer happens to me. Buber calls this experience becoming *aware*. Such is the awareness of which I speak here, an awareness born from silence, from listening.

This generative theme of awareness that arises out of silence is the discovery that all people who exist, but especially the silenced, are "words demanding an answer," incarnate words. As such, the awareness is political, and the discovery is that I am not alone in my silence. I belong—indeed, all of us in our diverse ways belong—to the culture of silence. The personal is indeed political—the me is you, the we is us. The moment of awareness is a concrete embodiment of Camus's "I rebel, therefore *we* exist."[14] It arises out of the sense of the outsider, and "therefore, the first step for a mind overwhelmed by the strangeness of things is to realize that this feeling of strangeness is shared with all men and women and that the entire human race suffers from the division between itself and the rest of the world."[15] Put religiously, the awareness of the word demanding an answer—the division Camus names—is the brutal fact of sin or evil or war. If I am silent, therefore people exist as separated from one another, especially in our systems, our forms, and our political structures. This is sin: not will to power or self-love or pride, not even distractibility, diffuseness, nor reliance on others for self-definition. Rather, it is sin at root as separation, broken-ness, and division. It is sister divided from brother, old from young, black from white, humans from earth. Awareness, there-fore, is awareness of the facticity of these divisions in our sys-tems and forms of education. It is educating and teaching that keep us from being who we are, from doing what we must do, from working to make the society less unjust, from being peace-makers, from forming and reforming the *Imago Dei*.

Analysis

As with the null curriculum, awareness is never neutral. Once we see, we can never not see. Awareness is like yeast. It grows and impels us to the educational task of analysis. The task of analysis incorporates the prior task of listening and refusing to be silent, and re-creates it in the form of questions put to our curricular environments, to our political and social systems, and to our ways of teaching.

The task of analysis has always been crucial for education. Analysis is the moment in teaching where the critical faculties of the mind are asked to concentrate all their force on the subject at hand. Analysis is one of the ways educators mediate the power to resist, especially too quick answers. Thus, critical questions of analysis are questions like the following: "Why is this so?" "What are the causes, especially the root or systemic causes?" "Who and what benefit from this situation?" "How?" "Is there any connection between what X says and what Y says?" "Are there contradictions here, and if so, why?" Critical ques-tions of analysis are *enabling* questions. In contrast to what Brian Wren calls "Guess-what-I'm-thinking" questions, critical questions are ones to which people can respond out of their experience. They are also problem-posing questions of the kind Paulo Freire has taught us, where people analyze the pros and cons of their own situations and thus invite further thought.[16] The task of analysis is fundamentally imaginative work. At the same time, it is also prophetic work. It begins and ends in envisioning; but in the middle are the works of interpreting, understanding, resisting, protesting, and advocating.[17] As such, analysis gives the lie to the charge that education in religion or education in imagination is mindless—strong in the heart, perhaps, but soft in the head. Analysis is the hardheaded component in educating toward re-creation.

When the task of analysis is brought to bear on situations that lead to and cause division among peoples and between humans and nonhuman nature, we need to make choices regarding perspectives and tactics (criteria) to guide analysis. Among the most instructive criteria for me are those Virginia Woolf named in the late 1930s in her book of essays entitled *Three Guineas*. At the time, a guinea was equivalent to one pound, one shilling. Woolf had been asked to contribute her guineas to educational efforts. Her response was a question of analysis: "How might I do this? How might I contribute to education yet remain a civilized human being?" Woolf decided, "I will contribute on the condition that if you accept my money, you refuse to be separated from poverty, chastity, derision and freedom from unreal loyalties."[18] In my view, a marvelous educational agenda: the refusal of division. Through poverty. By poverty Woolf meant enough money to live on, that is, enough to be independent or interdependent and nothing more; an early theology of relinquishment. Through chastity. By chastity she meant the refusal to sell your mind for money; when you have made enough to live on, refuse to sell your brain for the sake of money; an early exercise of ascetic, distancing imagination. Through derision. By derision she taught that, at all costs, laughter is better than being placed high on a pedestal. Laughter is preferable, especially a healthy laughter directed at oneself, which, although taking the self seriously, refuses to take the self solemnly. And through freedom from unreal loyalties, by which she meant we must rid ourselves of pride of nationality, religious pride, college pride, family pride, sex pride, and those innumerable unreal loyalties that spring from them and keep us separated, keep us from being citizens of one universe.[19]

At root, Woolf's agenda or criteria of perspectives and tactics is a religious counsel, a religious education. Poverty, chastity, derision, and freedom from unreal loyalties free the teacher from what C. S. Lewis called "the tyranny of the inner circle." They enable movement toward an ideal where there is no longer separation of people, no longer brokenness or division or bruisedness on any account.

If we were able to take on political awareness with its accompanying task of analysis it would mean agreeing to be responsible for bringing a new world into being, of re-creating the environment. And through such analysis, we could move from political awareness to a third generative theme. It would not, however, be a theme characterized by action. Instead it would be one founded upon sorrow.

MOURNING

The generative theme of mourning is a station, a stopping point, a necessary passageway between awareness and action. John Keats has described it as,

> Most like the struggle at the gate of death
> Or liker still to one who should take leave
>   of pale, immortal death
> And with a pang as hot as death is chill
> With fierce convulse, die into life.[20]

Mourning is the moment in education where teachers and learners are called to die into life. For if we grant, even for the sake of argument, that education is to attend to (to listen) and to tend (to care for) the outsider (the stranger, persons of every class, race, country, and religion no matter how divided from one another); if we grant that education is to be a work of love; and if we grant that education is to be designed and formed from a base that incorporates and takes seriously the experience of all peoples, then much of our present limited concentration and practice—our subtle suggestion that this or that particular approach, whether North American or middle-aged or male or Christian is normative—calls for a tremendous shift. It calls for a navigational change, a different course/course/curriculum where education results from the interplay of the perspectives and experiences of *all* people.

That call is voiced especially to those who have the power to make such change. And the best metaphor I know for this time of passage, this attending to the educational environment is mourning: discarding what is no longer viable and no longer appropriate, and turning toward purging, enlarging, reforming and re-creating it. For mourning to happen, however, something must first die.

In 1942, a tragic fire swept a Boston nightclub called the Cocoanut Grove. Within thirty minutes 492 people perished. After the occurrence, Erich Lindemann interviewed survivors and bereaved, and gave us one of the first technical descriptions of what is involved in grieving or mourning.[21] Six characteristics were especially evident: (1) somatic distress; (2) intense preoccupation with the image of who/what was lost; (3) guilt; (4) a disconcerting lack of warmth; (5) disorganized patterns of conduct; (6) the sense one no longer fits. I find a remarkable confluence of these characteristics in teaching and learning, reminding us that the journey to understanding is not always filled with pleasure. Indeed, the journey is often necessarily uncomfortable, painful, and sorrow-filled.

Elisabeth Kübler-Ross continued research into mourning and grief and elaborated five stages that anyone who lives in a culture of silence will recognize: denial, anger, bargaining, depression, acceptance.[22] I think of my own denial after the awareness of my silence because of my gender. I remember my initial disclaimer that I had been a victim of curriculum decisions. I think of my own anger, as well as that of my women students. I recall not turning from it, but learning to celebrate it. I am empowered by Beverly Harrison's counsel about the power of anger in the work of love,[23] and by Augustine's dictum that hope has two lovely daughters, anger and courage. We utilize anger so that what must not be will not be, and we act with courage so that what should be will be. I am supported even by Chrysostom, whom Aquinas quotes: "Whoever is without anger when there is cause for anger sins."[24] In other words, I and others recognize mourning in a deeply personal sense.

At the same time, however, I know that mourning is not just personal, it is systemic, too. Therefore, I propose that educating in ways that are religiously imaginative, ways leading to re-creation, includes moving with entire communities—class, study group, family, resident population, or PTA—through mourning, in the knowledge that grief is caused by systemic loss as well as by personal loss. When we let go of old ways and old forms, we may need time to acknowledge their passing, whether that passing is of a textbook, a relation, a pattern of learning, a position of authority, or an institution.

Further (and here is a place that incarnate earth forms are instructive), the mourning of silent people and silenced systems, the mourning for lost procedures, patterns, forms, and systems echoes in the planet itself, waiting to see what we humans will do. The rest of creation joins us, groans and travails, as with the great mythical and religious figures we descend into hell, make the passage down into grief and darkness on our way to light. The Christian Creed says of Jesus, "*Descendit ad inferos*; he descended into hell, into the depths." So must we all.

The bodiliness of the generative theme of mourning is also instructive. In religiously imaginative teaching, concepts, ideas, and beliefs surrounding mourning and death are particularly widespread. But mourning is more than concept: it has the character of ritual, a ritual of conversion and repentance where the work is literally putting off the old "man" and reknowing, re-cognizing mourning not as a topic of learning, but as the essential content, process, stuff, subject matter in all learning.

Letting Go

The educational task rising out of mourning is the task of letting go, a task similar to the moment of release described in chapter 2. The difficulty of the task ought not be minimized. It is extraordinarily difficult to change a person, let alone an entire system. Nonetheless, if we are able as educators to empower one another to let go of old wineskins (old methods, models, ideas), we find that our hands are free, no longer clutching and holding on. Then, with free hands, we can proceed unencumbered to enter and to dwell in the fourth generative theme: the strength of the moment of bonding.

BONDING

All teaching is a work of bonding, of mutuality, of communion. In teaching we engage with other people, with material, with ideas, and with environments. As I have tried to show in previous chapters, the nature of teaching is to be relational; communion is an integral and organic element in the teaching activity itself. Given where it is situated in this paradigm, that is, emerging from the themes of silence, awareness, and mourning, another facet of bonding becomes evident. The essential element of bonding in this paradigm is that "bonding" means bonding with the forgotten persons, the unremembered material, the dormant ideas, the unfamiliar environments. As already mentioned, bonding is a power of the weak, of the stranger, of the outsider. It is no accident that women throughout the world today choose *bonding* along with *networking* as central metaphors. As women, our political and social styles are characteristically mutual, communal, interpersonal, relational. That organic and feminist character of bonding provides a singular clue for curricular re-creation.

Study with me for a moment several examples of woman-bonding. First are the songs. In "Bread and Roses," we sing, "No more the drudge and idler, ten that toil where one reposes,"[25] asking for a common involvement in work. Holly Near sings, "We are young and old together, and we are singing, singing for our lives; we are gay and straight together, and we are singing, singing for our lives; we are rich and poor together, and we are singing, singing for our lives."[26] Cris Williamson sings, "Lean on me, I am your sister; believe on me, I am your friend."[27] Woman-bonding is also evidenced in feminist history: the Pankhursts, Sojourner Truth working with Sarah and Angelina Grimke, Elizabeth Cady Stanton and Lucretia Mott. Bonding is present in the lives and activities of all these women. Then there are the novels written by and about women. In the stories about the Bennett sisters,[28] Shug and Miss Celie,[29] Liz and Eleanor and Isabel,[30] and Meg, Jo, Beth, and Amy,[31] the theme of bonding is present. Then, too, bonding is present in religious history: Eve and Lilith,[32] Mary and Elizabeth,[33] Ruth and Naomi,[34] and the great Hindu goddess Devi, who embodies the theme of bonding in her own person, worshiped as Kali, as Maya, as Shakti.[35]

We women are justly angered that so little of this history and imagery is known. Nevertheless we are remarkably instructed by them. They dramatically teach the capacity for human relationship, the capacity to be sisters not only in one communion and tradition, but throughout the world.

Understood another way, bonding is the assurance of the

presence of sisterhood in education, and an argument for its inclusion. And why sisterhood? We have had the ideal of brotherhood for thousands of years in religious life, in social life, in political life. It has been a good ideal, better than many. But the ideal of brotherhood is incomplete without sisterhood. It is sisterhood *in partnership with brotherhood* that is necessary in education if education is to move toward re-creation.

To be sisters and brothers to one another is a fully human and fully adult possibility. At best, being mothers and fathers is available to us for only part of our lives; and some of us will never experience it. But to be sisters and brothers is a vocation open to all, and sisterhood leads to this fuller humanity. Sisterhood: a rich, textured title of cooperation and interdependence, hallowed in orders of women—and not just Christian women in religious congregations, but in Hadassah by Jewish women, too. It is found in racial communities, especially among black women. It is also a term we use when speaking of the planet, discovering, as Chesterton once remarked and as Francis of Assisi knew centuries before, the earth is not our Mother; the earth is our Sister.

Reform

The above ideal of bonding is worthy of the teacher's work, indeed of education as a whole. But like the generative themes preceding it, bonding requires a task. Bonding challenges us to undertake the task of *reform* (redesigning and reshaping) *in the light of* the demand that bonding makes. To return to the insights of chapter 2, bonding demands the reforming of subject matter. The system of clues, or subject matter in the first sense, must be shaped in the light of bonding's mutuality. The meanings beneath the subject matter must be held tentatively, with teachers and teaching communities creating ever-expanding circles, which are always able to include one more. The relation between teachers and students (the human subjects) must continually be reshaped toward the ideal of bonding and away from domination. Bonding must challenge us to reform the control, mastery, and oppressor attitude of humans toward planet earth. Perhaps most starkly, the study of the lives of all peoples, especially the outsiders, must impel us to reform our understandings of the Ultimate, the Holy, the Unnameable. As do all genuine tasks, the task of reform offers risk and loss. The final, yet most creative and creating, risk of reforming may be to replace the old Image of God. The Images of God we have entertained in the past may be too narrow and limiting to serve as the Ground of Being for a people and a world waiting to be transformed into a new creation.

In 1952, Sophia Fahs, whose entire lifework was one of re-forming in the light of bonding, wrote something of a credo. "The total cosmos," she said, "is one interdependent unit, down to the tiniest protons and misons and photons in the cosmic rays. Altogether, we are one unified cosmos."[36] What Fahs anticipated in her sense of the essentially companionate character of the universe was the centrality of bonding in education. The word *companion* is especially revelatory here, meaning not only one who associates with or lives with another, but also meaning, etymologically, "with bread." For only when we meet together to break bread, share bread, and be bread for one another, will we be able to "companion" one another. However, we cannot in any profound sense be companions until we have reformed the curriculum to include the experience and understanding of one another as we educate. When we move toward that inclusion, then we shall be able to rest in a last theme, born out of bonding. We shall have entered the moment of birth.

BIRTH

Communion and bonding are essential to engender birth. The physical manifestation of this in plant and animal life is obvious. The poetry surrounding human sexual intercourse is a reminder that human lovemaking is directed toward something being born—either in the relation itself, or in the new life that may issue from it. Put another way, making love is a creative and re-creative work, a work of artistry and imagination that has as its inner dynamic the possibility of birth. To give birth, we must first have bonded with another.

As with other themes in this paradigm, outsiders, particularly women, have extraordinary knowledge of birth. Indeed, birth may be the quintessential outsider theme. Rosemary Ruether's re-discovery of a 1923 work of feminist economist and philosopher Charlotte Perkins Gilman illuminates this insight. Gilman writes about two fundamentally different life orientations; one is based on the crises of male experience; the other is based on the crises of female experience. Gilman contends that the pivotal experience for men is death; but for women the pivotal experience is birth. Gilman writes:

To the death-based religion, the main question is, "What is going to happen to me after I am dead?"—a posthumous egoism.

To the birth-based religion, the main question is, "What is to be done for the child who is born?"—an immediate altruism . . . The death-based religions have led to a limitless individualism, a demand for the eternal extension of personality . . . The birth-based religion is necessarily and essentially altruistic, a forgetting of oneself for the good of the child, and tends to develop naturally into love and labor for the widening range of family, state and world.[37]

Much education seems to me death-based, in the sense that competitiveness, narrowness of vision, and refusal of admittance to the multitude has similarly led to a limitless individualism and a demand for the eternal extension of personality. We have not developed naturally toward love and labor for the widening range of family, state, and world. We have not contemplated the "terrible things." Thus, we have kept ourselves not from the pain of death, but from the pain of birth. However, if birth is admitted as a generative theme central to education, perhaps even as a direction for education, we can learn new ways to explore the uncharted places in our curricular geography.

The first thing birth teaches us about educating is a different sense of time. Human birth takes nine months; It refuses to be hurried. For teachers who find themselves pressured to "do it all in the fourth grade," this can be a liberating notion. Semesters and grades and courses can be understood as openings and beginnings where seeds are planted. But the moment of revelation comes in its own time, in the healthy unhurriedness of birth.

Human birth also takes place in hiddenness. Even though our sophisticated technology gives us all kinds of clues about the future, the daily movement toward birth happens in darkness. All good teachers have some sense of this. A teacher who can serve as a model is the wise and hard-working L. C. Moffat of Emlyn Williams's great play, *The Corn Is Green*. We eavesdrop as

Moffat reads the young miner Morgan Evans's first attempt at writing:

The mine is dark . . . If a light come in the mine . . . the rivers in the mine will run fast with the voice of many women; the walls will fall in, and it will be the end of the world. . . . So the mine is dark. . . . But when I walk through the Tan shaft, in the dark, I can touch with my hands the trees, and underneath, where the corn is green. . . . [38]

Moffat then works with Evans in a metaphoric, comparative process, trying to discover where her own teaching might bring life to this slowly greening human being.

Finally, because human birth is, by definition, a bearing, it poses demanding questions for education. What are we baring? What are we baring or revealing? What are we asked to bear in the work of teaching? Birth tells us that we bear bodiliness, enfleshment, new life, passion, emotion, feeling, blood, water, and pain. Birth tells us that we bear human selves, and that here is work worthy of teachers: giving birth to other selves; even giving birth to our own selves, for the sake of one another and for the sake of the earth our home; giving birth to forms and systems and structures that make life humane for the peoples of the world; even giving birth, in Meister Eckhart's description, to the God waiting to be born from us, for we are all "Mothers of God."[39]

Celebration

When we allow birth to teach us these things, the educational task demanded by birth will not only be clear, but we will also discover our own bodies and the body politic engaging in the task spontaneously, the task of celebration. Perhaps we will even find ourselves rejoicing in the acknowledgment that all birth calls for joy, festivity, and happiness. As with all birth, we will know the moment of birth in education, and for a while will be able to forget education's pain and suffering, and revel in the knowledge that genuinely new life has entered the world. We may have to wait for such celebration for long years; yet at some deep level, at some profound place, we will be willing to wait, because we have been touched by imagination and impelled by a vision: of *shalom*, of justice, of peace, of love; of the inclusion of the outsider, the stranger, the forgotten ones. And how do we recognize this vision? What does it look like? At the end of chapter 4, I sketched the features briefly. But here is its full face:

And then all that has divided us will merge
And then compassion will be wedded to power
And then softness will come to a world that is harsh and unkind
And then both men and women will be gentle
And then both women and men will be strong
And then no person will be subject to another's will
And then all will be rich and free and varied
And then the greed of some will give way to the needs of many
And then all will share equally in the Earth's abundance
And then all will care for the sick and the weak and the old
And then all will nourish the young
And then all will cherish life's creatures
And then all will live in harmony with each other and the Earth
And then everywhere will be called Eden once again[40]

II. TEACHERS

7. A Pedagogical Model

At the beginning of his remarks on teachers in *Life in Classrooms,* Philip Jackson makes the observation that in teaching, as in all other crafts, there are masters from whom apprentices should learn.[1] John Dewey had made a suggestion similar to Jackson's years before. Remarking on the benefits to education of a master-apprentice relation, Dewey said that:

beneficial consequences extend only to those pupils who have personal contact with gifted teachers . . . the only way by which we can prevent such waste in the future is by methods which enable us to make an analysis of what the gifted teacher does intuitively, so that something accruing from his or her work can be communicated to others.[2]

The presentation of teaching in this chapter arises from the kind of possibility Dewey and Jackson suggest. It is also offered to give form and flesh to chapters 1 through 6 by describing a master teacher at work, Mary Anderson Tully. This gifted woman, with whom I once had the privilege to work, incarnated subject matter in a way that truly revealed it. And I am only one of many for whom she mediated the grace of power. Her death in 1981 did not end the effect of her teaching, and one of my hopes for this chapter is that the personal contact many of us had with her in the forty years of her teaching will not be, to use Dewey's term, a "waste." I was lucky enough to be her apprentice for a time. Now I would like to share the benefits of that apprenticeship with others.

BEGINNINGS

During 1969 and 1970, under the auspices of the Religious Education Department of Union Theological Seminary in New York, I was able to observe, participate in, analyze, and reflect upon the teaching activity of Mary Anderson Tully as her graduate assistant, colleague, and associate in the course "Art and

Christian Education." From my point of view, apprenticeship is the vehicle that provides the best and most adequate understanding of the pedagogy in that course. I will describe my apprenticeship and her teaching in this chapter, and in doing so, suggest it as a pedagogical model for the field of education in general.[3]

The best introductory word to describe Mary Tully's teaching is *aesthetic*. The essence of the aesthetic is that it cannot be captured or capsulized. It is always susceptible to further interpretation. Rather than being oriented to aims, goals, and objectives, the aesthetic flourishes in a climate where one waits to see what will emerge. Before analyzing Mary Tully's teaching style and its implications for all teaching, I will describe my own initiation into it as well as a number of the situations that led me to realize I had made a genuine discovery about teaching.

The first conscious awareness that I was in the midst of something new, though as yet indefinable, came during the morning of our second or third class session in October 1969. I had arrived two hours before class to help set up materials. On that particular morning, Dr. Tully told me that we would be painting with water and colored inks, and that we would need live flowers for the session. She did *not* suggest that the flowers would be models to copy. My immediate assignment was a trip to the florist for a bouquet of flowers. My directions were concrete. I was to find several large circular flowers, several with angular lines, others that grew together on one stem or stalk but at different places along the stem, and others that grew clustered together. I was to choose vivid colors.

Tully could have told me to buy chrysanthemums, pussy willows, and gladiolas, but she did not. Without realizing it, I had been introduced to the language of art and given my first experience in looking with the eye of an artist. In the class session, this experience was taken a step further. Each participant (and in most classes I was one) was directed to select a flower and to take a few moments to look at it. Then Tully gave her first direction: "Find three colors in the flower at which you're looking, and using three different colored pens, draw the shapes made by those colors." I panicked. I had a *yellow* chrysanthemum in my hand, and it was, or so I thought then, just *one* color. But then I began to look, and gradually I began to see. There were indeed several colors: white-yellow and yellow-white, grey-yellow and yellow-grey, green-yellow and yellow-green. I began to capture the shapes of these different colors and to express them on paper.

Later in the day, I brought the last two pussy willows back to my apartment and set them on a small table next to the television set. I had again the experience of seeing something that I felt I would not have noticed before. The lines of the pussy willow were situated in space almost parallel to the lines of the television aerial. But the pussy willows' lines, although immobile, were obviously *alive*.

Something had happened to my characteristic way of seeing, but I did not yet know what it was. Questions began to arise for me in a somewhat formless, intuitive way. They had something to do with the way I was seeing and the things I was seeing. Could it be that communicating in shape and color and line was in some way analogous to communicating in language? Did our propensity for labeling things short-circuit the process of seeing? What had Tully done as a teacher to widen my visual experience?

A second element in my apprenticeship was the sheer amount and kind of preparation for each class session. Tully referred to it as "setting up the environment." Although I had been a school teacher for seventeen years, I had never prepared so hard or so much for any class, often beginning on one Tuesday afternoon for the next week's Tuesday morning session. But this preparation was a different kind from what I was used to in graduate study. I could not help comparing it with my own teaching experience and with other graduate assistant work. Tully's preparation involved not only setting up materials to be used in the particular session, but often the preparation of alternate materials as well. It involved careful consideration of the personalities in the group and the way they might react to particular teaching strategies. It involved study of the work that had been produced the week before so that we could be aware of what each student had done thus far, of where she or he seemed to be in understanding the process engaged in, and of the different levels and degrees of the students' involvement. We often planned the session down to the number of minutes, including the five minutes for coffee at the beginning.

It was not long before I began to see the relation between this readiness or preparation and the use of time in the teaching situation. For, when class time came, the material close at hand created an anticipatory atmosphere. Paradoxically, however, as we became involved in each new medium as a vehicle for expression, the completely prepared material became the catalyst for the new, the unexpected, and the unprepared. Instead of taking time to get water, the water got splashed on paper, and the time was spent in seeing what the water did: how it ran across the paper, how much or how little was needed, how it mixed with ink, what happened when it was stirred with paint. The emphasis was on involvement with the material, truth to the material, and discovery of the limitations and capacities of the material. I found myself meeting clay and crayon and more abstract artistic concepts, such as form and line, on their own terms, and I felt myself developing a new reverence toward them. I could not manipulate them; I had to be in relation to them. At the same time, the lack of emphasis and often the actual *deemphasis* on representational art (on drawing or making copies), freed me from anxiety about producing likenesses and left me open for the unexpected. When I tried to imitate models or had preconceived ideas, my work was disastrous. When I opened myself to the materials and resources, letting myself play in the situation, I made discoveries.

Once more, questions began to arise. We were having class, giving and receiving directions, explaining events, and supplying information, as all teachers do. Then what was different? How much did the preparation determine what happened? Was all this preparation necessary? What was it in the climate of the class that had been evoked by the preparation? And what exactly was meant by "setting up the environment"?

My third and most vivid memory of those first months as Tully's apprentice comes from the contrast I experienced between her class and other classes. Although I had been teaching since 1952, I had not begun to complete my doctoral studies until seventeen years later. In that 1969 to 1970 academic year, the fourth of my graduate study, I was finishing courses. Thus, besides assisting Dr. Tully, I was engaged in a good bit of additional academic work. The contrast between work with her and my other work struck me more vividly as the semester progressed. In all of my graduate work the pattern had been similar and predictable. Courses were centered around printed and written material. They consisted of lecture and discussion in varying proportions. They usually required term papers, and they were notably discursive, rational, and cognitive. Feeling was not a constituent of the courses; and if I had been asked to describe what they felt like, I would have had to say that they could be "felt" in an objective, detached way. On Tuesday mornings, however, that entire academic pattern was turned upside down. The classes did have verbal elements: prodding, explicative, instructional, and discursive talk. But these elements were balanced by long, contemplative sessions where we worked with intense involvement to express in media other than words what it was we were perceiving, understanding, and feeling. There were also discussion periods, sessions on the meaning of art, as well as reflective sessions near the end of the term where we attempted to separate and pull together the strands of the course—process, artifact, reflection—but these always came after the experience and sometimes long after it.[4]

My first reaction to this contrast was that I felt cheated. I can remember being irritated that nowhere along the line in my graduate studies had the feeling part of my humanity been consciously a part of my formal education in the way I was experiencing it in Tully's class. My second reaction was that deep springs were being released in me—by this teacher in this situation—springs that seemed to be of such a depth that I could only call them religious. It was at this point that my educational questions began to be clearer and my conscious explorations of the nature of teaching began to take form.

In the first place, I had to ask whether I agreed with Smith that "teaching is, above all, a linguistic activity,"[5] or with Aschner that "teaching is essentially and typically verbal,"[6] even when verbal was widened to include gestures, tone, and facial expression. It seemed to me that Tully's teaching, indeed, had verbal components, but that they were always pushing beyond themselves. What was the deeper meaning of the discourse in Tully's classes? What was being said *under* what was being said? Was it the *use* of language that differed? And were seeing and feeling and expressing as much an *essential and typical part* of the situation as the verbal activity?

Second, I found myself asking about the nature of the climate that was created. Far less emphasis was placed on end product than was placed on the process of producing and on the quality of that process. The teacher was present with a kind of active passivity that included a strong element of anticipation. "Find the form" and "see what emerges" were constant directions to students. In my view, climate is intrinsically related to the themes of incarnation, revelation, and power. This sort of climate has been aptly described, in another context, by Shumsky as one that

encourages the learner to rely on and utilize his or her potential, not to be bound to the concrete model, but rather to dare grope toward the creation of new and not predetermined knowledge. It is a climate which nurtures power to learn and create beyond the boundaries of the safe familiarities of the present and the predictable, and sparks in individuals the desire to outreach themselves.[7]

Most important, however, we were engaged with the feeling element in human experience. We were being given the opportunity and the tools with which to form the feeling element (or pole) of our intelligence. How Tully did all this, I did not know; and I could not foresee what she might do in any given situation, since intuition seemed to be a strong factor in the process in which she engaged. But I could observe, react, record, and analyze.

THE CLINICAL SITUATION

A number of questions had now emerged for me as paramount. I found that, often before the fact, I was beginning to refer to Tully's teaching as *aesthetic*. Yet I knew little, theoretically, of the nature of the aesthetic. Hence, I began to do some background reading while continuing my activity with the class. John Dewey's *Art As Experience* proved helpful in relating artistic and human experience.[8] This was immediately engaging for me in view of my understandings of revelation. Dwayne Huebner's discussion of teaching valued as aesthetic helped to center my educational questions, particularly through his contrast of aesthetic valuing with technical, political, and scientific valuing.[9] Ernst Cassirer[10] and Suzanne Langer[11] helped me understand art in relation to symbolization and form, although Langer was the primary theoretical support because of her interest in art as the creation of perceptible form which expresses human feeling.

At the same time, my questions were as practical as they were philosophical. I felt that my sessions with Mary Tully were exposing me to an incarnation of the theoretical material I was learning through my reading. My hunch was that a set of unique elements existed in Tully's teaching that were aesthetic and religious at the same time. Therefore, I knew that my task was to search for those elements, to analyze them, and to try to synthesize them into what I hoped could be conceived of as aesthetic pedagogy. To complete my task, my next move was to arrange for a clinical situation in which to examine my hunches.

Since the course would be taught again in the first semester of the following year, I asked Tully if I might make a conscious analysis of her class at that time. She agreed, and with the cooperation of her departmental chairperson, C. Ellis Nelson, it was decided that I would again act as graduate assistant in the course and be responsible for taping class sessions, individual conferences with students in the course, and any other pertinent sessions we might deem advisable. In my view, this decision gave flesh to John Dewey's counsel to find ways of capturing what great teachers do. In the next part of this chapter I will refer to much of the data I recorded. My second source of data comes from notes I took from my vantage point as assistant in the course, from conversation with teacher and students, and from my own observations.

The framework of the course and its participants are simple to describe. The three-credit course met once a week for two hours. There were eleven sessions between September and January. Seven students were enrolled, and each student had a one-to-one conference with Tully at midsemester after five sessions, and again at the semester's end.

None of the students were art majors, although one did have a good deal of instruction in art. Three had worked previously with Tully in an art fundamentals class, and three others had no art except for a single undergraduate course. Six were full-time students; one was part-time. All were young adults, graduate students in their mid-twenties. Four were women; three were men.

I found out this time what I had not known the first time around. The course was meticulously planned months in advance. Beginning in May, and extending throughout the summer, Tully prepared materials, searched out bibliography, and mounted exhibitions that would be ready as visual supports for the course in the fall. My own first conference in preparation for my work as tutor took place in May. At that time, Tully explained that we would be studying three artists in the fall: Graham Sutherland, the English painter whose great tapestry hangs above the altar at Coventry; Henry Moore, the sculptor; and Ben Shahn, the U.S. artist and social critic. We would not be studying them as art historians might, however. Instead we would be taking them as "points of departure" from which students could operate as makers and learners by becoming involved in processes similar to the ones the artists themselves engaged in. Since I was not an art major, and my main interests were philosophical and educational, Tully accepted the responsibility of selecting the substantive material of the course. Finally, it was interesting to me as apprentice to discover that the same course I had recently completed as a student was not being taught the same way twice.

In reflecting on Tully's work, I realized that my questions fell into three areas. The first two were antecedent and observable and could be more or less directly examined: First was Tully's use of language in the teaching situation; and second was her preparation of the environment. The third area was consequent and far less easily probed, but it had been the overwhelming element in the class from my point of view: the engagement with feeling. What actually happened in the class occurred in the interstices between these three areas. Yet what "happened" was never predetermined. In fact, my impression was that Tully's style of teaching intrigued me precisely because of the highly paradoxical situation where the unexpected, the unconditioned, and the genuinely novel was *revealed* in a richly planned and structured context.

Therefore, in reporting on Tully's pedagogy, I do so from the starting points of language, the environment, and the engagement with feeling and experience.

LANGUAGE: THE VERBAL AND BEYOND

It would be both naive and simplistic to take the position that language is not essential to teaching. Nevertheless, when Mary Tully taught, we her students found ourselves questioning its use as the dominant and often the only tool in the teaching situation. That few teaching activities can be carried on without the use of language is, I assume, self-evident. But to focus on language as the main instrument of communication, without the qualifying and complementary aspects presentable by other human, bodily activity—earth forms, embodied forms—seems to me deficient. Even more problematical is any point of view that fails to see language in tandem with what is necessarily beyond it, whether the latter is *pre*verbal or, as with much that is religious, *supra*verbal. In reflecting on Tully's use of language in the teaching situation, these considerations were uppermost in my mind.

Tully used language, as do all teachers, to instruct, to clarify, and to tell. In contrast to other courses, however, Tully's instruction, clarification, and telling always took place *after* the fact. For example, before the initial class session she explained to me that she wanted to make distinctions concerning the *language* of art (space, line, form, shape, color, planes, background/foreground, positive/negative) and the *roles* the students would assume (creator, maker, viewer, contemplative, critic, learner, teacher, reader). With the students, however, her approach was different. "Instead of telling them the difference," she explained to me, "they will *be* each of these things."[12] Her procedure was to give the group three different points of departure (for example, color, shape, space), asking each person to create a collage from them. Only after the collages had been made were the concepts *verbally* introduced, providing the students with a base in experience from which to understand the more conceptual data. For me, Tully's procedure embodied the incarnational, learning circle illustrated in chapter 3, a movement from concrete experience to reflective observation to abstract conceptualization to active experimentation.

When Tully approached Graham Sutherland, the first of the three artists to be studied, her procedure was similar. Tully explained to me that she had two points of special concern, the artist's biography, and the process the artist went through to create. Individual students had volunteered to report on Sutherland's biography; Tully was to introduce the students to Sutherland's process in a studio class session. When she did so, she explained, "There is one very important strand in Sutherland I'm going to emphasize, and the work we're doing this morning is the beginning of this. But I don't want to verbalize about it and make it abstract and unreal." She then led the students in a series of exploratory sketches, working from a natural object to help them create a symbol. She did not engage in verbal reflection on the symbol until the student's own bodily initiation into the process had been completed. With Mary Tully, the teacher, the word was always being made flesh.

Tied to this procedural element is a phrase or term in Tully's teaching vocabulary that has stayed with me through the years, one I have already used several times in this work (see chapter 6). It is the term "point of departure." Whenever a student was expected to produce an artifact, that artifact was related to some point of departure: a rock, a piece of bark, a live model, a theme. Tully did not encourage students to work apart from the actual world of humanity and nonhuman nature. Instead, she rooted her teaching in the concrete, the present. Her instruction would be accompanied by such direction as, "I want you to remain faithful to the object you're using this morning as a point of departure." And, when a student presented an initial series of sketches or finished artifacts to the class, Tully stressed the necessity for the students to reflect, as she did, in concrete terminology. "Vital, dramatic, stark, refreshing, quiet, clean," were the kind of descriptive words spoken by students in such reflective sessions. (We could never have gotten away with, "That strikes me as an eschatological manifestation of an ultimate, yet normative life event."—valuable as such an observation might be in other contexts.)

In retrospect, I realize that student experience never took place without conscious recognition of what was before us. But, over and over, what was before us was transformed by our efforts to capture its form, color, and inner reality through art. In that way, whatever we were studying revealed itself to us in the dimensions that existed below its surface.

Before long, this kind of procedure made it obvious to me that Mary Tully's teaching word was always complemented by sensory experience. We did not only hear, we engaged in tactile experience with materials; and inevitably we were able to see, because we were guided to do so. I have already alluded to my own experience with flowers as an illustration of the deepening of perception. As Tully's apprentice, I found others expressing in their reflections experiences similar to mine.

The structure of Tully's emphasis on visual experience gradually became clear to me. She would explain to students that she assumed they were problem-solvers and that when solving problems in her classes they would be creating visual symbols. At the same time, Tully also explained that the ongoing creation of visual symbols needed verbal reflection during the process at certain points. In order to move from point of departure to completed artifact, one necessarily used words. At times, these words were at a minimum. At other times, particularly where a student felt he or she was not progressing, Tully encouraged the student to fall back on words to inform, clarify, and decide where the student was. Even in such a case, however, words were directed to solve problems visually.

On other occasions, visual symbols provided alternate ways of learning, communicating, and expressing oneself. When Tully explained that visual material was present "in order to provoke and evoke and generate," I could confirm this by my own experience and by that of others. One student told us in an individual conference that previous to participation in the class (where he had begun to work with vivid blues, reds, and greens, and had created his own prints and paintings,) he had seen only "in black and white." Now, he discovered, "I see in color."

It made sense for Tully to explain to the class that what was happening was "training the eye, making the eye more sophisticated. It's capricious, it's not discriminating, it's nonselective, and you don't believe that you see what you think you see." It made sense for students on the highly personal level, because they could say of themselves as one did, "My eyes are on a different level than before . . . in the park . . . there are so many more objects that are alive now." It made sense on the level of creating, where students produced artifacts by looking at natural objects. Finally, on the level of human meaning, Tully confirmed that human life and human being are much more than can be said.

For me, a critical element in this class was that it provided a pedagogical model illustrating the difference between knowing about and knowing. Many of us already possessed a theoretical understanding of knowledge as an embodied human activity. But in Tully's class we saw what knowledge as bodily activity looks like, feels like, and how it comes about: the incarnating of verbal forms and embodied forms and earth forms and forms for discovery. Thus, although students knew *about* Graham Sutherland and Henry Moore and Ben Shahn, and although students knew *about* painting and sculpture and the artist as social critic, they did not necessarily *know* that subject matter. But by being placed in a situation where they themselves were makers in a process, producing artifacts, and working as these artists had worked, the students came to *know* them, to *become* them. It was this which gave Mary Tully's teaching, to use a phrase she herself used, "some kind of inner integrity." We were *doing* what we were studying.

Equally important was Tully's stance concerning the place of student learning and the function of subject matter, issues central to this book and to teaching as revelation. "The real teacher," she said, "is one who is excited about someone else coming to know something, but who doesn't do it for them. Automatically, you use analogy or you demonstrate or you use illustration, but you let them come to the knowledge by themselves." Tully did not think of subject matter as input or predigested information to be transmitted; her stance was to see subject matter as that into which one plunged, something that one *did*, "and as you do it, meanings emerge, connections are made between your experience and what it is you're encountering." Meaning, then, became that which was discovered and revealed in the situation. Meaning was end-point, rather than starting-point. It was under—not on—the surface. It was revelation. And although it soared beyond the verbal, the arrival at meaning, when couched in language, indicated that the verbal (the word), had served its purpose, taken its proper role, and been confirmed. When Mary Tully taught, words became incarnate and dwelt among us, and we beheld their glory.

THE TEACHING ENVIRONMENT

It is not unusual for educational literature to speak of the teaching environment and to speak of the teacher as the one who sets up that environment (i.e., that place where learning can occur). An analysis of Mary Tully's teaching reveals a particular angle of vision that confirms the literature and also furthers the argument of this book. Tully's unique vision enabled her to design the environment in a way that allowed students to *be* where, in fact, they were. That Tully thought of herself as one who set up an environment was evident from her remarks to students, and from her description of herself: "My main job is to set up an environment and expose you to something. But I'm not really *teaching* you. In this field, the field of art, you really learn by yourself and from each other."

Tully's description raised the following question in my mind: "What exactly is meant by *the environment*?" I have already remarked on the sheer amount of time involved in preparation, what Tully referred to as "seemingly a lot of detailed drudgery." Nevertheless, I realized that the so-called drudgery paid off, that the environment was much more than well-prepared materials.

Crucial to Tully's teaching, and one of her basic suppositions, was the belief that the environment itself could educate if it was properly set up—Eisner's "implicit curriculum." It needed, however, to be done consciously and with a great deal of *care:* care in the sense of precision and attention to detail, in the placing of table and chairs as if one were preparing a stage setting; care in the sense of a loving regard and solicitude. In Tully's class, the environment was planned, directed, and allowed to speak for itself. But Tully's concern for space, her weekly transformation of the hall in which we worked (the school had no art room), also spoke of a relation to inner space. The concerned attention to outer space, the *feeling* of space cared for, created the students' fundamental starting point each week. The quality of the environment enabled them to move inside themselves and be comfortable with the innerness they discovered there.

The balance of freedom and control Tully established made for a paradoxical situation. Students would remark how highly structured the sessions seemed to be. And they were. On the other hand, Tully made the point repeatedly that no predetermined response was expected. As a result the anxiety over producing was removed as much as possible. As one student observed, "She just seems to expect that we can do it, and we do it." The atmosphere was nonjudgmental. Time was not wasted on subtleties, innuendos, and manipulation. For example, if a student was not committing herself or himself on paper, Tully would say something like, "Are you not being evasive?" or "Could you not make that line a commitment?" It was the nature of the environment that raised such questions.

In order to probe deeper into the concept of environment in Tully's teaching, I decided to rely on direct interview. I could see what happened *in* the environment, but I wanted to know what went on in Tully's mind as a teacher in preparing to set up the environment.

Part of the answer came in response to the question, "What would you say are crucial elements in your teaching?" She spoke first of *polarities* in her teaching, then went on to give an example of controlled preparation and flexibility. She began by explaining what preparation did *not* mean: "By preparation I do not mean stating the goals, listing the materials, or precisely scheduling the amount of specified output." Nor did she believe that preparation was for a specified response: "Many times we [teachers] *have* set up the environment, but it has been to manipulate, to determine a prepackaged response." Tully eschewed such preparation and went on to say,

By preparation I mean, in the first instance, previsualization. I previsualize. I see ahead of time what the hall, what the students, what the material may be like. I find myself summoning resources, thinking through sequences of events, such as the gestures of a model. I do not see the outcome, but I do see the situation as in a film. And *as* I previsualize, I start preparing, and previsualization and preparation go on in concert, simultaneously, like a director and a stage designer working together.

In other words, preparation does not mean inflexibility and an ordered structure superimposed on the learner. It means setting up an environment which stimulates—which appeals to the senses and intuition, and which evokes the imagination.

One of the elements that enriched the environment was Tully's reliance on play, often closely linked to surprise. In one case, students were asked to sketch from a live model and to try and capture the dynamic line of forceful human activity. To ensure this, Tully surprised the class by having three of the students don costumes, pick up imaginary weapons, then march into the class and "freeze" in dramatic pose. The element of surprise was closely linked to humor and provoked laughter, since all knew the "actors." Nonetheless, it helped the students get at the possibility of doing away with predetermined responses. Tully would point to the interrelation of surprise and humor, saying, "There must be humor. There must be an acceptance of wit on all parts; and there must be some times where the order is upset, and the rules of regular, machine-like life disappear."

Tully also considered the particular students with whom we worked. For example, in preparation for one session, she and I were trying to decide whether or not to display the evocative, deeply symbolic paintings of Graham Sutherland, which we had already discussed in detail with the class. We considered each student in turn and her or his probable response if the Sutherland paintings were in the environment. Would they be help or hindrance to student ability? Would they be so suggestive and powerful that they might cut off possibilities as yet unformed and unarticulated? We decided *not* to display the pictures. The pedagogical stance behind our decision was an element in the preparation of environment. Explaining it, Tully said, "My style is to ask a question which applies to subject matter, technique, or strategy. And the question always is, 'Who is the learner in this situation? On whose terms is this learning going on?' " Tully's preparation was always *for* the learner, *directed to* the learner, and done *in terms of* the learner. It was not done in terms of material she wanted to cover.

The correlative to (or opposite polarity to) Tully's controlled preparation was flexibility. Once everything possible had been done to prepare for the learning situation, flexibility allowed the teacher to rest on that preparation, to let things happen and not to be afraid of them. In other words, flexibility allowed the teacher to see what emerged and to rely on intuition. The balance of control and flexibility or intuition was a delicate one. In no way did it presume anarchy, a situation out of control. But, as Tully said, "If you don't have intuition operating, you're afraid of things changing, because you don't know what to do with a pattern that might shift." Paradoxically, without intuition and its flexibility, there was no control.

Another set of preparatory elements Tully cited in response to my question were *challenge* and *expectation,* which, like control and flexibility, Tully linked to the learner. "I think that the human psyche can make sense out of its own environment, and the environment around it. I act on that presupposition. I don't instruct them very much. I demonstrate, but I don't instruct too much because I think students can make their own sense out of things if they know that it's expected of them." It seemed to me that Tully was saying that human beings are by nature learning beings, and that the teacher's role is to catalyze this learning, remove obstacles to it, and enrich the stimulation that leads to it.

Preparation and flexibility, challenge and expectation, and the teacher's relation to the learner: These ingredients help set up the environment. Still something more was needed. For, as Tully explained, "these elements are chaotic, until the teacher makes a vital organism out of them, because that is what a teacher does. You take all the disparate elements in a situation, ask people to come, select subject matter, work with resources and budget and whatever kind of skill you have. These are disparate, nonrelated items; and the teacher has to make a living organism out of them."

To speak of creating an organism is a tentative entrance into the world of art. So I asked Tully if she would say that was what art did, too. In the back of my mind lay the question whether or not one might refer to her teaching as aesthetic, and this seemed the place to put it to her.

Tully responded that if teaching *were* to be aesthetic, then it would have to do something like she described—bring about ordered being. This was why, she added, one could not separate curriculum and teachers and learners and methodology and still have a living and breathing organism. Thus, if the course were aesthetic, it would be so "to the degree to which it is an organism, because it would then be life, and a number of fragmented pieces and seven or eight very different individuals are somehow in tune with the materials, and with one another, and with me." And, I added to myself, with life and with the universe.

We left the discussion at that point, but a number of factors had been clarified for me about the environment and its relation both to the aesthetic and to the religious. In the first place, a crucial aspect of the environment was that it *raised questions*. The questions were concrete, personal, and unique, such as my probing of why the environment seemed to be aesthetic. By this time, I had begun to suspect that this conclusion was not drawn from the fact that the course was an *art* course so much as it was the *way* in which the course was presented. Although weekly assignments were never made, students often left the class with questions and testified to attempts they made to answer them by working during the week. I could not help contrasting this question-raising environment with the answer-giving ones characteristic of the other courses I had taken.

Two other experiences kept emerging from the environment, ones more closely related to the religious. The first I saw happen repeatedly: A student would begin hesitantly with a new technique, become familiar enough with her or his materials to dare something new, and emerge with a totally unforeseen result—an experience I earlier described as incarnation leading to revelation. I found events such as this akin to birth and wonder, and I realized that William James had spoken of them long before in writing of religious experience:

A human being's conscious wit and will are aiming at something only dimly and inaccurately imagined. Yet all the forces of mere organic ripening within are going on to their own prefigured result. . . . When the new center of energy has been incubated so long as to be just ready to burst into flower, "hands off" is the only word for us; it must burst forth unaided.[13]

The second experience was that of failure. For no matter how much preparation had been done, one always faced the possibility that this time it might not work, this time the "new center of energy" might not "burst forth." The environment or climate Tully provided not only allowed bursting forth, it also allowed failure to take place without censure. I was struck by the human consequences such experiences of failure permitted.

If there is no solution, then no premature solutions should be tried; rather the human situation in its conflicts should be expressed courageously. If it is expressed, it is already transcended. Persons who can bear guilt and express guilt show that they already know about "acceptance-in-spite-of." The ones who can bear and express meaninglessness show that they experience meaning within their own desert of meaninglessness.[14]

THE ENGAGEMENT WITH FEELING AND EXPERIENCE

I do not think it a caricature of the graduate school curriculum in the humanities to describe it as a largely conceptual and verbal enterprise. The typical course is carried on almost completely by verbal interaction, is addressed to a body of subject matter contained in printed material, and obliges the student to submit a paper or papers as written evidence of her or his understanding of the field in question. Students must fit into that particular framework. Who students are, what they are feeling, and the nature of their subjective human experience, is not usually a substantive part of the course.

In contrast, a unique feature of Mary Tully's pedagogy was that feeling was *primary* in it. The engagement with feeling and experience, as Tully carried it out, is my basic reason for suggesting that her teaching was aesthetic. More accurately described, Tully's style was not only to engage feeling and experience, but to engage them in such a way that they were fused with the workings of the mind. "The difference between esthetic and . . . intellectual is . . . one of the place where emphasis falls in the constant rhythm that marks the interaction of the live creature with its surroundings. The ultimate matter of both emphases in experience is the same."[15]

Tully had a healthy respect for the way the mind works, and for the necessity of realizing that there is a point where the

rational and feelings dovetail. For her, feeling and thinking were
not separated in actuality; therefore, she did not separate them
in her teaching. In contemplating a print or reproduction, for
example, she taught that one first sees it and feels a response
to its impact. Then, if the person takes time to examine the art
work and to reflect on it, the normal consequence was, "You
find your feelings changed. The searching of the mind has
begun to enlarge, transform, change your feelings." It would be
the grossest misrepresentation of Mary Tully's pedagogy to think
that in it feeling was opposed to reason. On the contrary, feelings were taken seriously and consciously addressed as elements
in the process of learning. Seriously considering feelings meant
necessarily that the rational was involved, too. What was important, she told students, was "not only what you produce; it is
the way you feel, the way you think, and the manner in which
your idea and your feelings are related. I think that is our
business here."

Tully stressed this activity as particularly important in adult
life, lamenting the tendency in schooling to work on the intuitive
and sensory levels only with children, and to regard such activity as somewhat primitive and proper only to childhood. She
suspected that, in actual practice, most people involved in the
educational process believed "the epitome of maturity in education is to be a thinking type." Thus, Tully cautioned us that
"if you accept the idea too completely, you tend to cut off your
feelings." Therefore, and in contrast, Tully taught both that
human beings of all ages need to understand the feeling element in their existence and that this was especially appropriate
for men and women who were students of the humanities. Because she saw the question of art tied to the concreteness of
daily life, she saw art as "a corrective and balance to the other
(abstract and highly conceptualized) things students are doing."
Art kept the curriculum from being lopsided. "The curriculum
is overloaded in some other way if they [students] don't have it
[art]. Young people want something that will involve sensation,
intuition, and feeling." Referring to one of the men in the
course, an articulate English major who had admitted in an
individual conference that he wanted to relax and in this course
he could do it legitimately, Tully concluded, "We feel guilty if

we play too much, and sometimes if we play at all. There simply must be something that is a breaking of the pace, that touches another part of our being."

Such comments get at the aesthetic roots of Mary Tully's teaching. Like the philosopher Suzanne Langer, the way Tully worked with human feeling was to help students give form to such feeling. Tully related this to the religious: "I believe that your search for what is real, what is ultimate, is your religious process." Referring to the relation between the religious process and the artistic process, she continued:

I think your direct expression of this relation and the risk you take as you express it without evasion on paper week by week, without fear . . . is the walk of faith, true faith. Most of us can escape lots of other ways, but you cannot escape the discoveries which come from direct expression. You can diddle around and mix colors, but if you really try to be expressive, and to *give your feelings form,* I think you're coming very close to the nature of your own being.

Engagement with feeling and the aesthetic dimension are necessarily related, since it is art through which feeling is given expression. "The thing that makes our work or anything aesthetic has something to do with feelings, and allowing feelings to take form . . . feelings don't have form initially."

The basis from which Tully operated in creating opportunities to give form to feeling was human relation. That is to say, her primary attitude toward students was one that regarded them as fellow human beings. All other roles (such as teacher, student, master, apprentice) were subsidiary. This in no way means that Tully's teaching atmosphere was "folksy." But her attitude did create a basic security in which each person's unique inner life was treated with reverence, respect, and ultimate seriousness. She knew that each student had an ontological vocation to be a subject.

To relate to others in the class situation on such a human level presumes further attitudes toward the learner and toward oneself as the person responsible for the learning situation. As regards the learner, Tully said, "I believe that the human interior or psyche or depth is the locus, the anvil upon which one forges out meaning for oneself. I think the human psyche is mysterious. I think in and of itself it has a way of going about its own business." Trusting the human psyche to do its work, Tully provided a climate or environment of freedom (as described in the previous section) where it was able to do so: "Their [students'] interior life has a reasonableness. It has a way of operating; it does move when it's given a chance; it can learn from things around it. It must be given a chance to work out its own mystery."

Furthermore (with respect to the attitude toward oneself as teacher), just as the interior life and the personhood of the members of the class were constitutive of the course, so, too, was the teacher's (Tully's) personal reality. "I present my reality to them because one of my presuppositions is that the teacher has to have a reality, a confident reality; not be someone without flaws, but an individual, a maturing, changing person. I need to consciously present that to them, just as I need to have them present themselves to each other."

This presentation of personal reality to one another was dependent upon Tully's view of the nature of teaching, shaped by the discipline of art. Tully describes it:

Teaching is a living encounter with other human beings. The teacher is responsible for seeing that the environment is such that they can start learning by themselves. Art is one discipline which allows for directness and immediacy and where the possibility of pretension and escape is cut to a minimum.

In suggesting then that Tully's teaching was indeed aesthetic, I do so by reason of the serious engagement I observed in her classes with human feeling and human relations, which are primary elements in human experience. Tully's approach to experience was to address it as that in which human being is always engaged. Teaching and teaching art are grounded in this deep base of experience, and they are natural activities assisting human beings in addressing human experience. Speaking of students, Tully declared, "They can operate as self-learners, and their learning is not so much about art as such as it is learning *through* art. They are learning because they want to learn, on their own terms, and from whatever sources make sense to them. What I have to do is make my best guess as to what to put into the situation that will help them to make this sense."

Tully's best guess did not necessarily mean that the curriculum should be overhauled. But it did mean, for her, that the curriculum was a playground where students could really fence with ideas and decisions, "fence with material they've had before and come to terms with it—fence used in the play sense." As I have pointed out, Tully did not see her role primarily as one of being responsible for input. She was aware that students had a great deal of input from other courses, and consequently, she saw her role as being responsible to provide a time, a place, and a vehicle in which students could make sense of the input they already had.

Using the discipline of art as the basis for such teaching had a twofold effect. In the first place, it provided the kind of playground spoken of above. But secondly, and more important, it helped make sense out of experience. As Tully put it,

Art builds an opening,′ a new conscious opening into knowledge of yourself, and the world, and your own identity other than the knowledge you've had before. You are made to stand still, and somebody jars you out of your habits, and that's one of the reasons I teach the way I teach. . . . And, all of a sudden, you find yourself out in the sunshine, in a new world; a new world of feeling, and a new way of looking at things. You look at a bus differently, and at trees, and at flowers. And at life.

CODA

I would like to conclude this chapter, this memoir if you will, as I began it, by referring to John Dewey. For, to my mind, it is Dewey who best expresses the synthesis of affective and intellectual activity exemplified by Mary Tully. It was Dewey who explained why the work of an artist or an artist-teacher is not the denigration of thinking and speculative activity, but rather its completion. For Dewey, the idea that an artist does not think while a scientific inquirer does nothing else is the result of mistaking a difference in tempo and emphasis for a difference in kind. For the artist, thinking occurs through the qualitative media in which she or he works; while the scientific worker operates with symbols and mathematical signs. Furthermore, Dewey contends that an aesthetic quality must be felt in *all* experience.

Not only is this quality a significant motive in undertaking intellectual inquiry and in keeping it honest, but . . . no intellectual activity is an integral event (is *an* experience) unless it is rounded out with this quality. Without it, thinking is inconclusive. In short, esthetic cannot be sharply marked off from intellectual experience, since the latter must bear an esthetic stamp itself to be complete.[16]

If Dewey is correct in seeing this combination of the aesthetic and the intellectual as characteristic of all human activity, then aesthetic teaching, as I have described it in this chapter, provides an educational model valid for all teachers. And if teaching is an activity of religious imagination, as I have tried to argue in this book, then a model such as Mary Tully proves it is possible for all of us to incarnate subject matter in ways that reveal subject matter. We, too, can mediate the grace of power to human subjects as they engage in the work of re-creating the world.

8. AN ARTISTIC MODEL

The music makes me sing, in my searching
for answers to the big questions. I wonder
how the sparkle of mountains
relates to candlelight. And opera
seems a frivolity of celebration.
Where am I going?

To class and we dance and with puppets
we haggle over yarn and
who performs first.

But back to opera and that big question:
Significance!
Who knows where the time goes,
until the time is
Up
And I still can't get my kite flying.

Somehow the significance lasted despite
the paint I dripped, the tangled string,
the significance of frustration;
Acceptance . . .

In a festival of doing—striving
for, together. Laughter
in the glow of afternoon—wanting to Be there
as elves climbing Christmas
with trees of holly, candy, candles.

It makes our sense.

I dance in my humanity,
The clown sang so today,
For then the world's insanity
Skips briskly from our way.

People ask, "What happened in class today?"
"Everything, oh everything" and I hold up evidence in
silk-screened perception.

"Creative self," I say.
"Created self." I know.

DIANE LOCKWOOD

AN ARTISTIC MODEL

An adult woman close to finishing her graduate studies wrote that poem, attempting to incarnate in verse the experience she'd had in a course I taught entitled, "The Aesthetic and Religious Education." We can taste something of the flavor of that course by realizing that, by Lockwood's own account, it raised questions of meaning and significance for her. Somehow the course offered an occasion for acceptance-in-spite-of; somehow it chipped away at part of the world's insanity; somehow it was provocative enough to raise for those who were not there the question, "What happened today?" And somehow, Diane Lockwood and others entertained the possibility of meeting not only their creative selves, but their created selves as well. Wanting to *be* there.

In this chapter, I will talk about that course and describe it in some detail, fleshing out this essay on the theology of teaching with a second example of how religion, imagination, and the act of teaching can be brought together. The course is related to the work embodied in Mary Tully, and it is an attempt to put into practice some of the leads she offered me many years ago. But the course (and my relating it here) is also an attempt to describe that form for incarnation of subject matter, the form of art, which completes the forms named in chapter 3: verbal forms, earth forms, embodied forms, and forms for discovery.

Since the completion of my own apprenticeship with Mary Tully over fifteen years ago, I have regularly put my name next to a course description which reads: "The Aesthetic and Religious Education. This is a course exploring the arts *in* education, and the artistic as a quality *of* education. Participation in artistic activity is stressed; emphasis is on non-discursive learning."[1] First at Fordham University in New York, and over the last decade both at Boston College and at Andover Newton Theological School, with as few as four students and as many as forty-five, I have continued to explore the relations between religion, education, teaching, and the artistic. Sometimes the course has been tightly structured and relied on much verbal interchange. Alternately, in other years it has been looser, freer, and characterized by spontaneous and serendipitous play in almost every session. But almost always, as the class members have testified, the course has culminated in experiences that have enlarged vision and deepened insight.

In the next few pages, I will attempt to share some of the excitement and imaginative activity that have been part of this ongoing adventure. I will begin with the underlying philosophy of the course, move to a description of its basic design, and conclude by describing some of its results. In so doing I hope to present readers with an example of artistic education they might consider as possibilities in their own teaching. As I begin, however, I need to emphasize that I am not an artist by profession, but, like most of my readers, a practicing teacher. One does not need long years of training in art to bring the aesthetic to educational work: One needs only desire and the conviction that as teachers we are all artists, creating forms that enable our students to see and to live at deeper and more profound levels, levels that might accurately be called religious.

PHILOSOPHY: POINTS OF DEPARTURE

The starting point or philosophy behind this course is two-fold. First, and theoretically, the starting point is the philosophy of this entire book: Teaching and the education of teachers are fields where the religious quality intersects with education. The imaginative, viewed in this chapter as the artistic and aesthetic, is a dimension of both religion and education. If, as I have already noted, art is the creation of perceptible form expressive of human feeling,[2] then both religious forms and educational forms are especially appropriate vehicles for such expression. Religion, with its ties to creation and feeling, is the cultural vehicle that gives people forms through which to express their relationship to divinity. Education, with its focus on the intentional reconstruction of experience,[3] has relied strongly on form as well. But education, in contrast to religion with its stress on ritual and liturgy, has relied more on the creation of *conceptual* form and thus is in need of the more concrete and perceptible forms proper to art. From this, we may conclude that the field of teaching can only be enhanced by including the aesthetic.

The second starting point for the course has to do with understanding what constitutes a mature adult. The overreliance on psychology in our century has obscured the fact that integrity as the goal of psychosocial development (Erikson), universalizing faith as the goal of faith development (Fowler), formal operational thought as the goal of cognitive development (Piaget), and postconventional decision making based on an abstract concept of justice as the goal of moral development (Kohlberg) are only *interpretations* of maturity.[4] To these interpretations must certainly be added an exploration of artistic or *aesthetic* development, what Howard Gardner refers to as "full participation in the artistic process."[5]

In saying this I do not want to negate the findings of the developmental theorists (mentioned above), so influential in today's educational circles. I do, however, want to record the fact that in studying human development, (that is, human integrity or maturity) we have not generally studied artistic or aesthetic development as much or as carefully as we have studied psychosocial, faith, cognitive, and moral (decision making) development. We have certainly not celebrated artistic or aesthetic development, nor held national symposia to consider it. Because of this omission, we are in danger of assuming that we understand the nature of the adulthood toward which we educate children as well as adults. We are especially in danger of offering an image of the adult as an autonomous (read rational) person, so often proposed as a developmental ideal. That image needs re-evaluation, for it implies that one should be able to give up not only one's affiliations, but also one's sense of play and spontaneity in order to become a "grown-up," a separate and self-directed individual.[6] To offer the artistic as a way of learning, of knowing, and of valuing is a corrective to such assumptions. Art demands affiliation with the concrete material of the earth. It demands a sense of play. It demands that some moments *not* be productive. It is not for *use*. But it is also the nature of art *not* to provide or promote any one answer as *the* solution, goal, or definitive meaning of adulthood, as developmental work is prone to do. In art, multiform possibilities for interpretation *always* exist.

Advocating inclusion of the aesthetic is, in addition, advocating a special kind of healing needed in education, the healing of the split created by too-sharp divisions between the disciplines. In most educational circles, the danger exists of separating areas of study and people such as artists, poets, and mystics from other areas of study and people who may be referred to as scientists and thinkers (a separation that today's scientists are often among the first to challenge). Thus, we enter the course I am about to describe trying to build bridges between those areas too often kept separated. Happily, many of our colleagues in the sciences are engaging in this enterprise as well. In our course, we draw, for example, on such biologists as Lewis Thomas, who bring poetry and medicine together in a disposition of awe.[7] We make connections with writers such as Fritjof Capra, who, while searching for an image to capture the world opened to us by subatomic physics and its relation to religion and art, has settled on a metaphor of the world as a "cosmic dance":

photographs of interacting particles, which bear testimony to the continual rhythm of creation and destruction in the universe, are visual images of the dance of Shiva equaling those of Indian artists in beauty and profound significance. The metaphor of the cosmic dance thus unifies ancient mythology, religious art, and modern physics. It is indeed, as Coomaraswamy has said, "poetry, but nonetheless science."[8]

In similar fashion, John Dewey noted decades ago the error of separating art, science, and other modes of knowing. "Only the psychology that has separated things which in reality belong together holds that scientists and philosophers think while poets and painters follow their feelings."[9] Dewey goes on to say that there are "emotionalized thinking and feelings whose substance consists of appreciated meanings or ideas" in both art and science.[10] Teachers, as religiously imaginative actors and artists, must not only be wary of making this separation, but they must actively seek to remove such separations wherever they find them.

Finally, because I am a teacher of religion and education, the course is based on a set of assumptions not just about adults, but about adults studying in the fields of religion, theology, and education. Some students are *afraid* of the artistic, and therefore are hesitant about involvement in it. Far too many recall terrible incidents involving childhood forays into the artistic. For example, in the area of music, many students remember the experience of gustily and lustily participating in a class glee club, choir, or chorus, only to have a teacher whisper gently, "Don't sing, dear." Other students recall the equally devastating moment of holding up a drawing in first or second grade with the hope it will be displayed, only to be told to return it to their folder and try again. Nevertheless, as adults such students recognize that they were not at fault in such early experiences, and they are eager to overcome—even with some trepidation—their fear and tentativeness. They are ready to try out, finally, powers that may have been held in abeyance for years.

In contrast, other students who come to class are especially sensitive to the aesthetic, need artistic expression in their lives as much as they need food, and are aware of this need. They come, many of them, from having majored in fine arts or drama or dance in college, or from avocations and vocations as musicians, weavers, painters, or poets. These students see the course as an opportunity to integrate and pull together disparate elements in themselves and in their lives, as well as an opportunity to plan procedures for their own teaching work with others.

Most of the students I have taught, however, even if they do not articulate it, come because they have a desire for space: personal, religious, psychological, geographical, as well as the outer and inner space Mary Tully addressed so well. They need a spot, a place in the curriculum where they can integrate what they are learning in other fields. This is especially true when those other fields are characterized by the search for ultimate meaning, final destiny, and unconditioned reality, as much of theological and religious study is characterized. Because of this, I find that, like Mary Tully's, much of my role is

to help students, through art, to make some sense of the content they're already getting or have had. My experience has been that most of these adults have had so much input that has not been digested that it is really a form of indigestion. And they need an area where they can in secret, and at their own pace, without somebody bothering them, integrate some of this material.[11]

My own conviction is the same as Tully's. It has been borne out over the last decade with students similar to hers. Though I would not for a moment advocate the aesthetic as the *only* course in a religious or humanities curriculum, I would fight for it as an essential course precisely because of its integrating, holistic, and digesting quality. The artistic in the curriculum provides an oasis where people can, in peace, let their understanding, their intellect, and their feeling come together without pressure, but with support from within the institution where they are learning.

DESIGN

The design of the course has varied somewhat through the years, but one basic assumption has held: Participation in the art form under study is essential to understanding the aesthetic. No art form has ever been chosen and then simply talked about; it has always been *done* as well. Some years this participation has been minimal and discussion has been predominant, although not exclusive. Other years, discussion has been almost nonexistent, and participation has been central.

The best approach, on paper, is a blend of the two—not always achievable as smoothly as I or the students would wish. However, the original purpose and description are generally presented at the first meeting something like this: "The purpose of this course is to provide understanding of, participation in, and expression through various art forms. For some forms, the professor will take responsibility. For others, class members will be asked, either individually or in teams, to choose an artistic form, research it, and develop a process to engage the other class members in the form. At various times, class members will act by taking the roles on the artistic circle: as creator, as performer, as audience member, as critic. Attendance at all class sessions is expected, since they form a key part of the course, and are its focal point. Class members with expertise in various forms may be called on as resource persons in these forms, but are encouraged to choose for presentation areas with which they are not familiar. It is strongly recommended that all class members keep a journal to record their impressions for themselves as the term progresses."

Over the years, I have shared the teaching role in the course with students, asking them to choose and present "artistic forms," a phrase which we have corporately agreed can cover a wide variety of possibilities. We have engaged in dance, choreography, poetry, creative dramatics, song, sculpting, silk-screening, puppetry, fairy tales, and cooking. We have baked bread together, we have clowned together on busy streets, we have molded clay into a plethora of forms. We have learned how to make and fly kites. "What does kite-flying have to do with graduate education?" one woman was asked. She replied, "Everything." And then went on to recount the religious depth the course had given her and to speak about how the awareness of herself, of others, of the divinity became clearer as her own gifts and talents were discovered—even needed—in the process. Diane Lockwood put it differently:

> And I still can't get my kite flying.
>
> Somehow the significance lasted despite
> the paint I dropped, the tangled string—
> the significance of frustration.
>
> Acceptance for okay-ness.[12]

Acceptance. Understanding. Of what it is to fail. And of what it is to soar.

These forms, new or unexplored to many when presented, are then developed in a way that enables class members to take on the four artistic roles. When someone designs a session, is "on" for the day (sometimes two are "on," hence Lockwood's "haggle over who performs first"), she or he is engaged in the role of *creator*: responsible for putting the matter together in new ways. When the person demonstrates and presents, he or she takes on the role of *performer*, with the rest of the class acting as *audience members*. When the class begins to take part, however, *each* member becomes a performer, which helps to alleviate any feelings of self-consciousness, since we are all in it together. Finally, each person is requested to take the role of *critic* by assessing the class presentation *following* their own.[13] The point in all this is that once one has designed and presented, he or she is in a better position to critique.

I would be less than candid and lacking in sensitivity if I did not note the considerable risk such involvement in the artistic roles entails. One man, reflecting on his experience at the end of the course, put it this way:

> I am more comfortable in the safe modes of academic endeavor, among the papers and the exams. It is a hard thing to be creatively dramatic. It brings tears to my eyes, sometimes, and feelings of tightness and embarrassment at unaccustomed actions in the sight of others. What are *they* going to think? Worse yet, what am I going to think of myself when I realize that all these unexplored possibilities are dormant in me? And that (dramatics) is just one of the forms we explored. Each one brought its own peculiar terrors along with its joys. I guess I realized again how far we drive the child in us under cover, and how hard it is to trust the flow that pulses in and through us.[14]

Besides offering engagement in the four artistic roles, I have discovered that the course can often be anchored around three conceptual poles: *word; world;* and *wisdoms. Word* is an appropriate starting point because of the heavily verbal nature of much schooling, particularly the teaching act. (I should note, at least in passing, that some years I have presented an entire two-hour class in and on silence, silence itself being a provocative artistic form.) I regularly draw on Langer's distinction between discursive and presentational forms as the starting point to explore words, since it is her way of analyzing verbal symbolism.[15] As noted in chapter 3, discursiveness is that quality of verbal symbolism which requires us to string out our ideas even though their objects are related all at once. Discursiveness is what requires us to treat serially what happens simultaneously, placing our words one after the other, as clothes on a line. The issue this raises initially is whether what is knowable is confined to the requirements of discursive projections. If it is, what can be known can also be said. If it is not, then there are innumerable possibilities of meaning beyond the limits of discursive language.

Langer adopts the latter position. While affirming the necessity of language for human exchange, she points out that its characteristics necessarily limit it. She distinguishes this limiting, discursive kind of symbolism from a second kind, which she refers to as *presentational* symbolism. (An important naming; she does not speak of *verbal* and *nonverbal,* since the latter would preclude poetry, drama, the novel, liturgy.) This second symbolism is one where a simultaneous, integral presentation is made all at once, wholly, as distinct from the serial projection of discourse. But the significance of this understanding for the students with whom I am working is the connection with both religion and education. In the first place, *word* can be understood as not only discursive, but also as presentational; thus the *artistic* forms of words (poetry, drama, novel, fairy tale) can be studied as educational vehicles. Religiously, however, especially in Christian, Jewish, and Muslim traditions, the word is also central. For, as I tried to point out in chapter 3, the word is not only a verbal utterance we humans speak and through which we communicate; the word and language is a milieu in which we dwell and which reaches its fullness as the incarnation of human being, an incarnation of subject matter and of human subjects who matter infinitely.

World is a second conceptual pole in the course. The understanding of world here is of the earth, the stuff of which the world is made. In this course, I underscore the point that the artistic is a primary human way of establishing relations with this world-stuff: clay, pigment, water, color, line, paint, sound, body. Much of our education tends to cut us off from our bodies. But that may also be true of religion. In our everlastingly talky educational and ecclesial circles, the bodiliness we must call on to shape and mold clay, to dilute and mix color, to harmonize and project sound, and to dance with freedom and ecstasy is often minimized. A course such as this, however, necessarily emphasizes world and our relation to it. This emphasis is manifested not only in the times we design form together in the classroom, but also in the yearly experiences of going outside the classroom to sketch, to do rubbings, to fly kites, to discover earth sounds, to fill a silence. Because the work outside the classroom lies in the realm of creating form, however, it goes beyond the knowing of earth forms stressed in chapter 3. Here the earth is partner in the act of creating new form, of bringing earth into the creative activity to make what has never before existed in this particular way. And finally, knowing through world is even more congenial to presentational symbolism than are words. Thus, the educational impact of such knowing widens our concepts of rationality and understanding and intelligence, for knowing through the world's symbolism is as much directed to the *forms* of meaning as to the content. Knowing through the world brings much which has been relegated to the world of "emotion" or "play" within the compass of reason and intelligence, and thus encourages participation in the meanings the world *is,* as well as those toward which the world *points.* One student, a man of forty-five, wrote:

> The process required that I go outdoors, perceive something in nature thoroughly, enough to get some relation with it, and then, through the disciplined structure of a poem, express what I had encountered. The "something in nature" turned out to be the strong bark of an oak tree, which I attempted then to express in the following:
>
> Fibre
> Rough-layered,
> Stretches, routes, contains.
> Tough, enduring shell of life
> Bark.
>
> It may not be great poetry; on the other hand, I surely know more about bark than I would through many other processes, and not only more *about* it, but know *it,* itself. When I was with the bark, it gave itself to me, and through the poem, possibly to others.[16]

These, then (*word* and *world*), are the first two conceptual poles around which the course revolves. The third, *wisdom,* is of such import I shall treat it in a separate section.

WISDOMS

The third and final element of the course has been its wisdoms. In other terminology, these might be called results, learnings, conclusions, meanings, but I prefer the notion of wisdoms, because of the richness of that word and its multilayered meaning. To begin with, wisdom does mean learning, as well as the understanding of what is true, right, or lasting. But, playing with wisdom a bit, one discovers the Middle English *wisedom* and then the Old English root *weid.* And *weid* is "to see"; as the Germanic *witan* is "to look after" and "guard" (cherish?), and the Old German *wissago* is "a seer" or "prophet"; as the Greek *weid- os* is a "form" or "shape," an "idyll"; as the Old Irish *white* is "clearly visible." What is it that one sees after a course like this? What takes form, takes shape? What is seen, imagined? What becomes clearly visible?

Four wisdoms stand out: foolishness, creativity, wholeness, and worship. *Foolishness*, the first wisdom, is demonstrated in presentations such as fairy tale telling and making, puppetry, and clowning. Spending an entire semester on the artistic is a reminder that not all knowledge is for use, and in our culture that is undoubtedly foolishness to many. The artistic, the aesthetic, reminds us that the more-than-rational exists and that it nurtures and feeds the human spirit if we let it. But in the course there is also the foolishness of making a fool of oneself: trying something in front of others at which we do not come off as experts. For such activity, one of the guiding aphorisms of the course is a caution Corita Kent has used with her art students: "There is no win, no fail, just make."[17] So, together we agree to be fools in this class: We put on the patched pants and outlandish costumes of the clown, hold up mirrors for one another as we change our features (or often change each other's features) to make bulbous noses, purple eyelashes, and oversized mouths, imitate slapstick gestures and purposeless phrases. And in the attempt we gain the wisdom of our own finiteness, our limitedness, our foolishness in a symbolism simpler than discourse. As Lockwood writes,

> I dance in my humanity,
> The clown sang so today,
> For then the world's insanity
> Skips briskly from our way.

The second wisdom is our own *creativity*, which is made possible by the absence of pressure to win, and by the shared commitment to make, which tends to grow as the course continues. "I noticed," observed one doctoral student, "that as our class became engaged in the process of this course, a sense of community developed. We took risks in each other's presence and with each other's support. We became resources to one another as we encouraged and critiqued our performance."[18] That climate, that environment, is essential if the following conditions for creativity are to exist: (1) the *detachment* that is willingness to accept any outcome; (2) the *passion* that can be expressed in an unthreatening atmosphere; (3) the *immediacy of involvement* in a process along with the *deferral of satisfaction* that is almost always present in a two-hour segment; (4) the *letting the art work* (or object, or art process) *take over*—that is, allowing the internal drama to unfold so that one can *let the material be* what it must be; (5) the *relinquishing* of the urge to *control* and to be in charge.[19] And when these conditions for creativity do exist, one is able to come to a new seeing, a new understanding, a new imagining of oneself: "I gave myself and parts of me that were new to me to this class. My participation in the various classes was not outstanding, but it was outstanding to me. Me— who seldom did anything creative (other than having children); me—dancing around the room (at my age!); me—making a puppet (not a good one, but I made it); me—weaving and on and on; me!! And especially me! having the courage (no guts!) to teach a class with a new friend."[20]

The third wisdom is a sense of *wholeness*. Most times, graduate students work with words and with books. Although I go to great lengths in class to point out that dealing with the aesthetic, the artistic, the nondiscursive is *not* a denigration of the world of discourse and rationality, but a complementing of it, the sense of wholeness seems to come through more easily by helping the students encounter the material universe by working in the intuitive, the imaginative, and the perceptual modes more proper to art. I also try not to name the wisdoms for students as the course draws to a close. However, I must admit to hoping that such experience of wholeness will occur. For this reason, I cherish the end-of-semester response of the woman who wrote the following:

The course helped me to be integrated; it gave me an opportunity to use and develop my intuitive side while the rest of my courses demanded the activity of my analytical side. Religiously, this is significant for me because I believe in a holistic view of life; that work and play, joy and sorrow, day and night are all important parts of life, all equally important. I try not to divide the secular and the sacred; I try to live as if my life is a sacrament. The integration of the aesthetic and the intellectual is part of the synthesis I keep trying to incorporate in myself.[21]

Finally, there is the wisdom of *worship*. Although the course is not a course on or about worship, it steals into the curriculum each year. At times, someone chooses to conduct a class on prayer or meditation or liturgy. More often, there appears to be an appropriateness in choosing the form of worship as a closing to class. One of the most memorable of such classes was one where the artistic form chosen was food, and where together as a class, having been *(Been)* together for thirteen weeks, we made bread, butter, salad, and sweets in the course of the two hour session. Then we sat down to a shared meal, notable for bread, for wine, for community, and for the grace before and throughout the meal that acknowledged our dependence upon the divinity for those fruits of the earth and for one another.

REPRISE

Despite the extraordinary range of art forms and activities re-created in the course, two stand out as most memorable to the participants: the molding of clay and the experience of clowning. Over and over, when I meet someone who has been part of the class, and we talk about it, "Do you remember the time when we . . . ?" usually ends either with a reference to taking clay into one's hands and probing it in secret and in solitude, or to taking upon oneself the identity of the clown, and then moving outward, in attention to, and awareness of, others.

In both cases, as I have already suggested, the procedures we have followed have been fairly simple. With the clay, our first step is to take in hand a fairly large, one-pound lump of un-formed, unmolded, and unremarkable "stuff." We turn it over in our hands, throw it up in the air, pound it, pummel it, even fling it flat on a surface, and finally mold it into a sphere. The purpose of these first activities is to get to know the material, to establish a kind of communication and communion with it so that we can move on to the next step.

In step two we freely agree to blindfold ourselves in order to be better able to "find the form" within the clay. The directions are always simple and on the order of those Mary Tully used to give: "Within this lump of clay a form resides. What we are going to do now is find that form. But, in order to do that, we need to get our preconceived, visual notions of what the form looks like out of the way; we must allow the clay to lead our fingers and our hands. Trust that a form is there. Trust that it is unique. Trust that it waits to be discovered." Those directions are almost always enough to move people into a silent search—and silence is needed here—for the form dwelling within their clay. From then on, with only minimal comment and direction from me (for example, "Don't be too tentative. Use all of your fingers and all of your hands. The form is there, you will find it."), the person and the clay become known to one another, and eventually arrive at a time and a form of completion, rest, and resolution.

The activity of clowning is also fairly simple. We bring clown makeup and old clothes, gather for some brief introductory reflection on the history and meaning of clowning and our purposes in doing it now—as Carol Brink did in the passage in chapter 3—and then we apply the makeup and get dressed in our cast-off clothes. After that, we often gather for a sending-forth ceremony with only a few rules: Go out in pairs; go out in silence; go out as one who has freely received and now freely gives; go out in hope.

Both the clay and the clowning have an integrity in themselves, and when we have engaged with them or in them, a tacit knowledge of their greater meaning appears to be present. Often, people will attempt to probe the experience and its meaning toward the end of the class if there is time, but that is actually not needed. The making and the doing speak for themselves.

Nonetheless, I think it worthwhile to wonder why these are the two activities that people have named through the years as the ones most significant to them. I cannot help think that clay and clowning tell us something about ourselves and our world, especially since they are, at first glance, so different. For me, it is the apparent difference (actually only apparent) which provides the clue.

As I have worked with clay in the company of others all these years, I have come to know clay not only as the quintessential metaphor for teaching. I have also come to realize that clay serves as a form for a journey inward, a journey for oneself, in silence, where no right answers are necessary, where there is neither winning nor failing, but simply being creatively alive. At the same time, the journey with the clay provides the opportunity to discover the inner form of some other piece of creation and to touch—literally—what Gerard Manley Hopkins might have called the "inscape" of some thing.

In contrast, clowning is a journey outward, a form that allows people to leave the self-consciousness of their own persons and, for a time, to put on a mask of universal humanity. Wearing that mask as well as the clothing of Everyperson, people are able to go forth to others and to the world, bringing no preconceived and prepackaged ideas, no face to save, no need for words, but only the simple possibility of giving away the smallest but most precious gifts: food, touch, a caring human gesture.

Our world is incomparably complex and incomparably needy. Clay and clowning will not solve our problems. But they may give us clues to which forms are available to us as we try to incarnate subject matter in ways that lead to the revelation of subject matter. The search for forms may then make us aware of our form-poverty, our form-bankruptcy in the mediation of the grace of power. But if we are people who are trying to make the world more humane, that search cannot end. And in the continuing search we may even discover that we are helping recreate the world. Ultimately, that is the vocation of the teacher: to incarnate subject matter toward revelation and power, and thus to take part in the re-creation of the universe.

9. Invitation to Imagination

In chapter 7, describing Mary Tully, I offered a pedagogical model. In chapter 8, describing my own work with students, I offered a model based on art. In this chapter, I issue an invitation to teachers to create their own models, using their own capacities for imagination. Mary Tully is one teacher; I am another; and our truth to ourselves is to be the best teachers we can be. But such is true for all of us: We teach best when we are most truly ourselves. Thus, I extend here an invitation to imagination. I extend it to the individual teacher who is reading this book and who is asking, "If I were to put into practice myself some of what you have described here, what counsel would you give me? What paths might I follow?"

This chapter is a response to that question. I will attempt here to make suggestions appropriate to teachers who want to work out of their own imaginations. These suggestions are born from the major themes of this book: incarnation, revelation, power, and re-creation. I will return to the themes by way of recapitulation; I will also point out how they are related to the four forms of religious imagination. Each teacher's response will necessarily be idiosyncratic; nevertheless, some general principles or criteria can help guide us in the journey. I will be naming five criteria, which may also be thought of as paths to take or moments in which to dwell. Although presented in sequential order, these criteria are not only related to one another, they also necessarily overlap. I will also suggest exercises to accompany each criterion. In order, the criteria (paths) are: (1) take care; (2) take steps; (3) take form; (4) take time; (5) take risks.

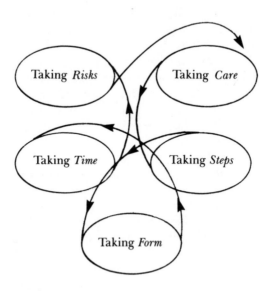

TAKING CARE

The initial criterion for any teacher is the criterion of taking care. The starting point of the teaching act draws not on material resources—those will come later—but on spiritual ones. Care is an attitude, a way of being toward the other, a decision in favor of reverence and respect. Taking care implies we will not hurry into the teaching situation. Instead we will be at pains to be still, to be silent, to be quiet and give ourselves the opportunity to survey what lies before us in the teaching activity. Care is what the Vietnamese monk Thich Nhat Hanh refers to as *Mindfulness*.[1] For teachers, care is the activity of being mindful of ourselves as teachers, of our students in their unique personhood, and of the subject matter that will be the third partner in our relation.

The most practical procedure I can suggest for taking care is to urge the disciplines of spirituality: meditation, prayer, periods of stillness. With my own students, before we engage together with subject matter, we often spend ten to fifteen minutes in quiet receptivity and awareness. "Sit back in your soul," I urge them. Then, drawing on the work of José Hobday, I explain, "And the way to sit back in your soul is to sit back in your body." Amazingly, they do. We sit quietly, and often it is possible to touch and feel and smell the quietude and openness that enters the room. After a brief time we are able to begin work together on the topic of the day. Invariably, those first moments create a receptivity to the material at hand.

Such an exercise is not limited only to teachers of religion or theology. I am aware of professors of management and physics who do the same. I am aware, too, of teachers of six- and seven-year-olds who also begin with such moments of taking care, urging the children to start the lesson by first going into their "heart room."[2] These moments are akin to the Jewish notion that on the Sabbath, the Creator of the world "draws breath." Taking care is the teacher drawing breath before the actual teaching activities begin.

Taking care does not actually start when we arrive in the classroom, however. It begins in our moments of preparation or, to use Mary Tully's term, our moments of previsualization of the teaching situation. I have often been struck by our (teachers') unreserved use of taking care *after* teaching, that is, our use of techniques for evaluation (or *post*visualization). The kind of taking care I speak of is the partner of that work, often left out in the rush to cover material. It is the work of using forms that create a readiness: using forms for *pre*visualization.

EXERCISES FOR TAKING CARE

Below are three simple exercises teachers might use to embody the moment of taking care. The first is toward care for ourselves as teachers; the second is toward care for our students; the third is toward care for our subject matter.

Taking Care of Ourselves as Teachers

Begin with a meditation, such as Heidegger's "Myth of Care." Care, it is said, was walking along the river one day, picking up earth and thinking, "Wouldn't it be wonderful if there could be human beings?" But because Care couldn't *make* human beings, didn't have the power, Care asked the Holy One to take the earth and breathe life into it. And the Holy One did. Afterwards, the following decision was made. Since the Holy One had breathed life into human beings, the Holy One would receive them when they died: the Holy One was where they were going. Because they were made from the earth, from the *humus*, they would be called *human*. But because Care had thought of them in the first place, Care would possess them all their lives.[3]

Such a meditation could then be accompanied by taking care to reflect well on the story, and then by asking ourselves questions like the following:

- Where am I, as a teacher, called to embody Care in the class I am teaching today?
- Where does what I am planning to teach today make my students more human? In what ways does it help them give form to their universe?
- Then, after reflecting briefly on each class member, ask: To what in my students' humanity will I address special care today?

Taking even three minutes to meditate on the responses to each of these questions can enhance the teaching activity immeasurably. In a brief space of nine or ten minutes, we will have taken care. (Throughout this book, I have attempted to provide many such resources for meditation, but I am not suggesting that teachers use *my* resources. However, I am urging the use of *some* to foster the meditation necessary to quiet us, to "still" us, in our preparatory moments and to help us remember what we are about. The best resources and meditations will be those we discover ourselves.)

Taking Care of Students

Care for our students is demonstrated primarily in our naming of the students. I would argue that regardless of class size, or age (adults, graduate school, little children), the teacher is responsible to know the names of every student with whom she or he works. If name tags are needed, so be it; a folded card at each student's place, set on top of the desk or taped to it can also be used. Whatever method is used, the point of the naming is to allow class members to be addressed as the persons they are, specifically, and not as generic or interchangeable "students." Being addressed as who one is enables a subject-subject relation, a communion of intersubjectivity, a feeling on the part of students that they are *seen*. Being addressed by name by someone who has taken the trouble not only to find out, but to remember what a student is called is a symbol of care for the student in the teaching situation. Such naming then creates the possibility of the student's willingness to accompany the teacher on the journey of learning, for the teacher has already begun that journey by, to use Kierkegaard's phrase, "going to the place where the learner is," and discovering the learner's name.

Taking Care of Subject Matter

Care for the subject matter can be addressed in a related way. One procedure I have found helpful is mentioned in chapter 3: personalizing the subject, as the Eskimo mechanics did airplanes, and as Progoff does in journal workshops. If the subject matter were to speak, what would it say of itself?[4] If it were to be in dialogue with us, what would that dialogue sound like? Taking a few moments to record even a half-page of dialogue can lead to revelation of subject matter we did not know we knew.

But these listenings will be in concert with the greatest respect we can show to subject matter: Finding out all we can about it. As reverent, careful teachers, it is our responsibility to do research, to study, to meet the material for preliminary conversations, to be prepared. Then and only then are we ready to introduce it to students, and to invite them toward engagement with it.

In these three brief exercises, which I hope would be catalysts for teachers designing their own, I offer taking care as a beginning exercise where the teacher uses each of the forms in the realm of imagination. In other words, taking care is a means of insuring that the teacher acts as a *contemplative*, intensely involved in seeing, attending, looking. It is a means of insuring that the teacher acts as an *ascetic*, who, by keeping a respectful distance, is at pains to do no violence to the student or the subject matter. It is a means of readying the teaching self to be a *creator*, by drawing together the elements needed in the act of teaching. And it is a means of moving toward making teaching a *sacrament*, an activity to be performed with the attentiveness given to ritual; a ground to be entered which is assumed to be holy.

TAKING STEPS

The teacher should receive the invitation to imagination as one would receive an invitation to a dance. I have already alluded to the dance metaphor in chapter 2, when I wrote that the steps in the paradigm for teaching (contemplation, engagement, form-giving, emergence, release) are not to be thought of as steps on a staircase, but as steps in a dance. The reason for the insistence on this metaphor of the dance may at first appear simple, but it implies a profound philosophy of education. This philosophy is based on the following assumption: The core of things is not substance, it is rhythm.

The influence of modern physics has helped teachers understand something of this philosophy, as we discover that all matter is constantly in movement. Modern physics has also assisted many in a return to the rhythms of the universe and to the startling rediscovery of the rhythm of our planet in its daily rhythmic rotation on its axis, as well as its yearly rhythmic revolution around the sun. These discoveries, in turn, return us to recognize the rhythms in our lives: the rhythm of our own bodies—our circulatory, respiratory, and digestive rhythms that keep us alive; our human living that occurs in a context of the ebb and flow of tides; the movement from autumn to winter to spring to summer; our rhythmic patterns of waking at dawn and resting at sunset. We are surrounded and held and nurtured by rhythm.

Rhythm in education is a theme with a rich grounding. In 1929, in the classic book *The Aims of Education*, philosopher Alfred North Whitehead described the rhythm of education as having three steps: romance, precision, and generalization or synthesis.[5] The first step is romance. In his view, romance is the moment of first apprehension, where the subject matter has the vividness of novelty, holding within itself unexplored connections with possibilities half-disclosed by glimpses and half-concealed by the wealth of materials. In this step, knowing is not dominated by systematic procedures.

In the step of precision, in contrast, the width of relationship is subordinated to exactness of formulation. Precision is a challenge to set some limits, to refine, and to deepen rather than broaden, at least for the time being. It is the challenge to stand back and contemplate, to reflect, and to ask serious questions, especially questions of analysis.[6] It is a challenge to recall that, if one is to reach the final step—synthesis or generalization, where the return to romance occurs—one must slow down and take time to reconnoiter. Classified ideas and relevant technique, which become coupled with the wonder and idealism of first apprehension (romance), are the rewards of precision.

Synthesis is the third step. It is the circling back stage—analogous to a dance, but a dance further along in time. Subject matter at this step is deeper and more beautiful, because this step is the coming together—the synthesis—of the loveliness of romance and the chastening, studied, ascetic attitude that precision has brought to the subject at hand.

Urging the teacher to take steps is the follow-up to taking care, in the sense that the teacher has now taken on the activity of teaching for himself or herself. The great temptation here, however, is to make the first steps in teaching ones of precision where systematic procedure dominates. My plea actually enhances systematic procedure. That is, if systems, procedures, processes, and tasks are to be learned, these are more appropriate and fitting *after* the step of romance; or, as described in the moment of engagement in chapter 2, after time has been taken for diving in, wrestling with, rolling around in, dialoguing, and interchanging with material which is not yet ready to be systematized. The rhythm of education must be respected; otherwise, the process will be short-circuited, and in danger of premature closure and conclusion.

EXERCISES FOR TAKING STEPS

The following three exercises can help us step both more lightly and gently, as well as more in harmony with the rhythm of teaching and education.

Stepping Around

Let the beginning of a teaching session be a "go-around." The students can be asked to do sentence-completion activities that directly address the subject, yet preserve the romance of first apprehension. If, for example, the subject for the day is morality, people might begin by giving names and then adding something pertinent to the subject. For example, "I'm Mary Jones, and one person who is a symbol of morality for me is——." or "I'm Dick Walsh, and one image of the moral life for me is——." or "I'm Annie Dillon, and one industry I consider moral in today's world is ——." The point here is that story, symbol, and image are ways of fleshing out the texture of a topic, and of teasing out the meanings in a topic. A "go-around" can preserve the richness of first apprehension. And, although I have used morality as an example, any topic might initially be addressed with such an exercise. For example, "I'm Susan Johnson, and for me faith is——; hope is——; war is——; adulthood is——"; and so on.

Stepping to the Rhythms of Story and Ritual

The steps in the rhythm of teaching can be applied to whatever subject is at hand, by way of assignment. For example, if a group is studying a novel such as *The Color Purple*,[7] we might develop a series of questions that moves through contemplation, engagement, form-giving, emergence, and release:

- As you **contemplate** the main characters, who comes first to mind?
- With which character did you find yourself most **engaged**?
- What did the author do to **give form** to this character?
- In what scenes did you find your understanding of this character **emerging**?

- As the book ends, what do you expect will happen next to this person? (**release**)

But the steps in the rhythm of teaching might also be used in the design of a story, which is our own story, perhaps even our own biography or life story, just as we have used it for the novel. In that case, the steps may be more intense and involving, and may call for more student engagement. For example:

- *Write* a story where the main character or characters move through these five steps.
- *Create* a story where you are the main character moving through these steps.
- *Tell* your own story in terms of this dance.

Again, the steps might be used in the creation of rituals, such as the Yom HaShoah ritual that commemorates the Holocaust, or indeed any ritual activity around a course of study, thus:

- What about the Holocaust do we wish to contemplate?
- With what aspects of the Holocaust will our ritual be engaged?
- What forms, shapes, patterns shall we use in designing the ritual?
- How and when will it be presented?
- What will be the hoped for or intended outcome?[8]

Addressing an event of the magnitude of the Holocaust is perhaps more appropriately done by taking time for the entire rhythm of teaching to unfold, rather than an immediate move to the how and when of its presentation. This in turn allows for romance, precision, and synthesis or for the rhythm that begins in contemplation and concludes in release.

Stepping Back and Forth

In the preparation and presentation of subject matter, we need, as teachers, to be sure of a constant forward movement and then return, if we are to be responsive to the rhythms of education and teaching. Therefore, in any previsualization of a class session, a third exercise is to imagine the subject matter both as presented to students and as received back from them. Rhythm demands this back-and-forth character; therefore, the time must be spent not only with teacher-talk, but with student-talk as well. But subject matter must also be handed over in a way that challenges students to hand it back. This is not done in the form of exams, or repetition; but as the result of the teacher who carefully hands something on, and then asks:

- Now, how might *you* pass this along?
- If you had been the one presenting it originally, what would have been your first step?
- In what ways would you formulate this question?
- To whom would you be willing to teach it, and what might you expect from them in return?

The point of this exercise is to help teacher and students move through rhythmic steps of forward and back, outward and inward, invitation and response, and to remain conscious all the while of the fact that teaching and learning are not linear and in one direction. Teaching and learning are organic, bodily actions, far more understandable in a context of repetition, return, diving into and pulling out of, and coming to points of rest and quiet before moving on to the next step.

These exercises, as with those offered under "Taking Care," use the contemplative, ascetic, creative, and sacramental powers of the teacher as resources. At the same time, they are also a set of movements forward along the paths of imagination, beyond mere reflection, and into the incarnational movements of human dance, human partnership, and human rhythm.

TAKING FORM

When viewed as an activity of religious imagination, teaching is the incarnation of subject matter that leads to the revelation of subject matter. Taking form, then, has much to do with incarnation—especially incarnation that leads to revelation. The criterion of taking form involves three decisions: to take form seriously, to take form as a starting point, and to take form into account. Without central attention to form, the teaching enterprise is in danger of failure.

The exercises below are examples of giving form to subject

matter in the actual teaching situation. However, any imaginative teacher will also be aware of form in two wider contexts.
These are the world itself, and the place where the teaching
occurs, usually a classroom. First, the imaginative teacher will
have an educated sensitivity to forms of learning and teaching
that are politically, socially, and economically oppressive. This
sensitivity will be characterized by the continuing movement to
look *for* and then *at* the dominant worldview, the set of values
and behaviors taken for granted and accepted as natural—that
which may be called the dominant ideology of a society—as
these are represented in the teaching situation.[9] Two examples
from previous chapters are pertinent here.

In chapter 5, "The Grace of Power," I wrote of the necessity
to cultivate the power of receptivity. Indeed, I name it first.
From one perspective, however, that power could be viewed as
passivity—indeed, as an ideological shoring up of the counsel
that poor people have always received from rich people, or the
counsel that oppressed people have always received from oppressors: "Don't hurry; you are asking for change too soon and
too quickly." Thus, it is important to be aware that what I, from
my North American, white, middle-class perspective, see as the
ability to sit still in a room and the necessity to take stock, take
account (take care), may have another rendering in another
social context. Citing the counsel here, I want to raise the caution that cultivating the power of receptivity may have to be
translated quite differently in another social location, or even
discarded. For some people, it may be too reflective of a world
view that deadens the spirit, although such is certainly not my
intention.

Another example is found in chapter 6, "Re-Creation." I begin the paradigm of that chapter with a first generative theme,
silence. I believe that theme is primary, and the meanings of
silence of which I have written have been worked on in a situation where black, anglo, hispanic, and Asian women have been
meeting together on issues of education and religion. The forms
of silence to which those four viewpoints attend have both sim-
ilarities and differences. Thus, the point I am making here is
the necessity for all teachers to work at awareness of the questions of how the *forms* of politics, economics, social location, and
ideology influence the teaching of any subject matter. I am also

arguing that the imaginative teacher include as many points of view as possible, as well as an ever-expanding awareness of the existence of opposing viewpoints.

A second, wider context, whose form has profound influence on the teaching act, is the physical and psychological form of the place where the teaching occurs—what Eisner calls the implicit curriculum—what might be understood by the term *environment*. We learn differently when we sit in straight rows looking at the backs of the heads in front of us than we do when we sit in circles, looking at faces. We learn differently when we are in a room with light and air—or are in the open air—than we do when we are inside a room with poor or no ventilation. We learn differently when we have color and decoration in our surroundings than when the walls are bare. We learn differently when a team of teachers, rather than one person, presents material to us. But we also learn differently depending upon our relations to the others in the situation, both the teacher and those who are our peers. We learn differently if the language of instruction is our second, rather than our first; if the examples used are not germane to us; if all the authorities who are cited as experts represent another sex or race or geography or even thinking pattern from ourselves. Each of these is a set of *forms*, and the teacher needs to take these forms with great seriousness as agents incarnating subject matter, in an implicit and subtle way, but nevertheless in a very powerful way.

EXERCISES FOR TAKING FORM SERIOUSLY

The most direct influence of form comes in the shape, design, and incarnation of the subject matter itself: verbal form, earth form, embodied form, forms for discovery, art forms. Therefore, the following exercises for taking form seriously draw on the two counsels: (1) Use all the forms of poetic speech on which you can draw; (2) use drama and mime in ways that incorporate body, earth, and the possibility of surprise.

Poetry

Use poetry. For example:

• Ask students to respond to questions in Haiku form.

- Ask students to find poems on whatever topic is being studied.
- Draw on the work of actual poets, such as Kenneth Koch.[10]

With reference to the first instruction, I have already shared Bill Maroon's classic,

> We meet awkwardly
> I invite you to walk.
> I find you dancing.

With reference to the second, I think of a class on World War I I attended recently (note the metaphor: It is often called "The Great War"), taught by Steve Cohen. Cohen distributed two poems. The first, "The Soldier," by Rupert Brooke, is a romantic view of war:

> If I should die, think only this of me;
> That there's some corner of a foreign field
> That is for ever England. There shall be
> In that rich earth a richer dust concealed;
> A dust whom England bore, shaped, made aware
> Gave, once, her flowers to love, her ways to roam,
> A body of England's breathing English air,
> Washed by the rivers, blest by suns of home.[11]

The second poem is by Wilfred Owen, a contemporary of Brooke. The poem, "Dulce et Decorum Est," has a starkly different first stanza:

> Bent double, like old beggars under sacks,
> Knock-kneed, coughing like hags, we cursed through sludge,
> Till on the haunting flares we turned our backs,
> And towards our distant rest began to trudge.
> Men marched asleep. Many had lost their boots,
> But limped on, blood-shod. All went lame, all blind;
> Drunk with fatigue; deaf even to the hoots
> Of gas-shells dropping softly behind. . . .[12]

The form given to the same event—war—renders the event with extraordinary difference. Imaginative teachers might offer two such poems to classes and then invite students to search for similar pairs, in order to get at the many ways of looking at any subject matter they are teaching.

In my own classes, I have often used the work of Kenneth Koch, a New York City poet, who has written about his work in teaching poetry to grade-school children in poor sections of the city, as well as to nursing home residents.[13] Koch gives creative directions to his students. He tells them, for example, to write lies (it is a wonderful thing for a child to get permission to lie, even briefly), to write wishes, to write dreams. One of his richest suggestions, one I have often used, asks participants to complete the phrase "I seem to be ———, but really I am ———" with a word or phrase. When I use this, I direct them to fold the paper, unsigned, and place it in the center of the room. Another class member chooses one of the papers and then reads it aloud with reverence and with care. As people sitting in a circle read a paper they have chosen from the larger pile, one after the other, the exercise invariably has two results: (1) It creates a community from what had been just a group; (2) it helps participants realize that they are far more alike than they are different. The anonymity allows for a wide freedom of expression, since people often write what they are reluctant to speak aloud.

Drama and Mime

It is a rare subject matter that cannot be learned through pantomime, embodiment, and creative dramatics. Most teachers are aware of that, but feel constrained by time. Yet the use of drama "fixes" insights in ways that accompany and enrich conceptual material. A presentation of *Fiddler on the Roof*, for example—or even a few scenes from the play—might teach more about the pain involved in commitment and conviction than a more discursive course. *The Roar of the Greasepaint, the Smell of the Crowd* or *Gideon* can teach much about the nature of dependence on the Holy One. As an example, teachers can consider the following passage from Paddy Chayevsky's *Gideon*, then go out and find plays that speak to the subject matter at hand, and produce them or read them together.

The Messenger: O! Gideon, would you have your God a wandering magician, slapping a timbrel and kicking his heels?

Gideon: Do not rise in wrath against me, sir.

The Messenger: I am not in wrath. I am plainly confused. And sore at heart. I have loved you and you have turned your back.

Gideon: I do find you personable, sir.

The Messenger:	Personable! Gideon, one does not merely fancy God. I demand a splendid love from you, abandoned adoration, a torrent, a storm of love.
Gideon:	*(With almost unbearable kindness.)* I'm afraid I'm not the splendid sort, my Lord. You want a less moderate man than I. I'm sure you shall find one soon enough, for you are an attractive God, and there are many who will love you vigorously. I'm sure of that. (He offers his hand and smiles disarmingly.) Come, if I have given you some hurt, then clasp my hand and say that it is over with.
	(The Messenger cannot help but be amused by this ingenuous fellow. He clasps Gideon's arm.)
The Messenger:	I shall make you love me.[14]

The revelation toward which such incarnation of form might lead is the depth of subject matter beyond and below the surface; depth open to human beings especially through the forms of poetry, song, sorrow, beauty, gesture, and most of all, other people. Taking these forms seriously gives teachers new opportunities to draw on their contemplative, ascetic, creative, and sacramental imaginations.

TAKING TIME

If the incarnation of subject matter is done with care, that incarnation can lead to revelation. In chapter 4, I described the nature of that revelation in some detail. Here I wish to note more of the practical accompaniments of teaching toward revelation. They lie in the criterion and the counsel: Take time. For revelation is gradual unfolding in the sun, inevitably, necessarily, as tomcats stretch; revelation is closely related to human birth and does not happen except in its own time; revelation cannot be guaranteed; revelation must be waited upon. Waiting for and upon revelation implies a willingness to dwell in patience with subject matter, even to see the values of darkness and unclarity of which Robert Graves writes:

> He is quick, thinking in clear images;
> I am slow, thinking in broken images.

He becomes dull, trusting to his clear images;
I become sharp, mistrusting my broken images.

Trusting his images, he assumes their relevance;
Mistrusting my images, I question their relevance.

Assuming their relevance, he assumes the fact;
Questioning their relevance, I question the fact.

When the fact fails him, he questions his senses;
When the fact fails me, I approve my senses.

He continues quick and dull in his clear images;
I continue slow and sharp in my broken images.

He in a new confusion of his understanding;
I in a new understanding of my confusion.[15]

EXERCISES FOR TAKING TIME

For the teacher, the interpretive keys for learning how to take time so that revelation might be fostered are found in self-conscious reflection, questioning, and probing the images of temporality. The exercises that follow are designed to help teachers become involved with each of these areas.

Self-Conscious Reflection

I use different "talking papers" to help teachers probe the meaning of revelation in teaching. One of these talking papers has five questions, each with enough space after it for the person to take notes, and then to engage in conversation with another student or teacher or with me. These questions are as follows:

- Have you had a major moment of revelation in your life in response to teaching? If so, describe it.
- What did you learn?
- How did you learn it?
- What difference, if any, did it make in your life?
- Has it made any difference in your own teaching?

Although in my experience teachers' answers to these questions vary, most teachers do respond that they have discovered revelation happening to them in two circumstances.

The first circumstance usually took place when teachers were themselves students, and a teacher *took time* with them, saw them as individuals, recognized the possibilities in the work they had done, and became catalysts to reveal them to themselves. In my view, these are examples of indirect communication. Content was not delivered; instead, these people as learners were delivered to themselves.

The second circumstance or situation that teachers responding to the above questions refer to concerns their own teaching. Their accounts tend to center around the times when they used forms for discovery, times at which the forms they used to incarnate subject matter did not predict what the outcome would be. I think, for example, of how a sixth-grade teacher introduced her geography class to caves. She did so by re-creating her classroom (environment) by turning it into a series of caves (by turning over furniture, by darkening the room, by asking the children to exercise their imaginations). As the teacher tells it, the learning about caves was far greater than anything she could have prepared from the textbook.

Questioning

In addition to self-conscious reflection, exercises can be directed to questions and questioning. If it is true that the place where the learner is—as I proposed in chapter 4—is the place of the question, then, as teachers, we need to probe the meanings of questions and to create for ourselves and our students a repertoire of kinds of questions. The context of learning to question is best described by Rilke's well-known passage:

Be patient towards all that is unsolved in your heart and try to love the questions themselves like locked rooms. . . . Do not now seek the answers; that cannot be given you because you would not be able to live them. And the point is, to live everything. Live the questions now. Perhaps you will then gradually, without noticing it, live along some distant day into the answer.[16]

Once that context has been established, we can move on to levels of questioning and explore deepening levels such as those illustrated below:

Set One: Types of Questions

Informational   (listing data, facts, specific content)

Comprehension   (asking about the meanings of content)

Application   (asking for places where the content applies)

Analysis   (distinguishing meanings in the content)

Synthesis   (making connections about the content)

Evaluation   (asking for judgments about the content)

Set Two: Types of Questions

Receiving/Attending   (asking about awareness of a content)

Responding   (asking where the greatest interest is, about what is intriguing in the content)

Valuing   ·   (asking whether students accept, agree, reject the content, and why)

Organizing values   (asking students to reform the content on their own terms, with their own criteria)

Characterizing values   (asking students what their own approach to the content would be, how they would describe the subject matter at hand).[17]

Probing Images of Time

A third exercise is directed toward probing our images of temporality. It begins with the revelation of the great breadth of human meanings we possess for time itself. If the criterion being suggested to teachers is to take time, then it enriches the criterion to explore the implicit imagery of time in much educational thought.[18] The discoveries are illuminating.

As now practiced, much of education, especially education in its schooling form, concentrates on the future. The imagery of temporality is one of time as composed of past, present, and future. Its qualities are linear and spatial. The purpose of schooling is to build the future, to make the future, to create the future. The present is ours to *use* in order to be sure of a better tomorrow. Indeed, we train as teachers—too often—in order to recognize where our students are along this great continuum of time, and we share techniques and methods that enable us to move our students on to the next stage.

We are told that we most wisely "spend" and "use" and "manage" this precious commodity through our activity *in* time, by our doing, our being busy. It is much better, according to our folklore, to light one candle than to curse the darkness—much better to *do* something than just stand there. And more crucial, as teachers we are told that it is best to be aware, in every situation, of how to design and implement behavioral objectives, so that we can define and measure and evaluate progress. For, we are cautioned, if we cannot assess movement from present to future—to see where we have been and how far we have gone—we have not really taught and probably have not learned. Publish or perish, we remind young teachers in the colleges and universities. But above all things, keep moving—*act.*

Given such imagery of linear movement—and activity designed toward progress, success, accomplishment, and future—we understandably find ourselves very much at home with Lawrence Cremin's definition of education, and, as teachers, we find ourselves engaged in "the deliberate, systematic and sustained effort to transmit, evoke or acquire knowledge, attitudes, values, skills or sensibilities, as well as any outcomes of that effort."[19] That definition points to a guiding philosophy of education: Education is effort, activity, doing, work. When the evening of our teaching lives comes, we shall not be judged (as St. John of the Cross suggested) on love, on how we *were* with students; we shall be judged on what we have *done.*

Given the above imagery of time and its consequences, it comes as a shock and surprise for many teachers to realize that spatial, linear temporality, imagined as past, present, and future, is only *one* among many human images of time. We have been caught in a North Atlantic image of temporality; in our own ideology of time. Australian aborigines, for example, imagine time both as an experience of immediate, ordinary daily existence, and as an experience of "dreamtime," which includes not only events of the sleeping state, but also those events we anticipate, envision, imagine, intuit, and conceive.[20] In dreamtime, the aborigine often chooses to go "walkabout." In our more mechanical, measuring view of time, an elderly person may simply say, "I am eighty-eight years old." Among the Tiv people of Nigeria, however, to grow old is "to finish one's body."[21] For the Hopi tribe of North America, temporal thinking is so drastically different from the ideas of Western time that there are no divisions such as minutes, hours, or seconds.[22] In contemporary literature, writers of fiction have so shattered narrative, sequential temporality that Annie Dillard can write of "time in smithereens."[23] And at the heart of Western religious tradition, the Jewish symbol and practice of Sabbath presents an image of time where the central note is Presence and a Divinity of Presence, not of future. Indeed, for the Jews, Sabbath began as a response to the divinity being-in-time with humans; and thus, for the first Jews, Sabbath was "the Sacrament of Presence."[24]

Such understanding leads teachers to a meditative exercise: Teachers contract with one another to be silent together—in the present—to contemplate their own understanding of time. The point of the exercise is to balance and chasten our understanding of time by the four forms of imagination. For without such balance and chastening an overactive, effort-filled, hard-working, *doing* understanding of time will cut off the possibility of revelation occurring in teaching. We teachers can destroy the contemplative imagination by insisting on hurry. We can turn the ascetic imagination inside out, where instead of insuring students space, it becomes an intrusive, unwelcome probe. We can unknowingly eliminate the conditions of waiting and receptivity central to the creative imagination. If we refuse to "take" growing time, sleeping time, learning time, we shut the door on the sacramental imagination and cut off our students' capacities to discover the Holy surrounding them in everything. I am returned to such reflection (often with chagrin and embarrassment) whenever I reread a poem given me by one of my students. The student, Thomas Evans, was a man who, like me, had great affection for Martin Buber. Indeed, he titled his poem-request "After Buber," and the request pleaded for my allowing revelation not only to be in *its* time, but in *his* time, not mine. It said:

> Teacher, be consciously active
> In helping me select a human world
> Out of the "purposelessly streaming education
>   by all things."
> Yet cast but a glance—lift but a finger—
>   act "as though you would not,"
> For it is my mysterious personal life at risk,
> And I must direct the fashioning.

TAKING RISKS

The *Oxford English Dictionary* defines risk as "hazard, danger, exposure to mischance or peril." The major danger to which the risk-taker is exposed is loss. And yet, I offer teachers one final criterion to act as counsel and as catalyst to their activity: Take risks. Take risks even if they result in great loss. The vocation demands it. For teaching is the incarnation of subject matter that leads to the revelation of subject matter. And the true revelation of subject matter is the discovery that we, as human beings, are called to be subjects in the world. We are called to exercise the grace of power in the direction of re-creation.

For thousands of years the relation of risk-taking and loss has been with us, and history indicates tremendous odds against the risk-taker. But I would argue that the risk-takers are the ones who have contributed most to human re-creation and transformation, often—perhaps most often—under the risk of death. Regretfully, when the choice between gaining the whole world and losing one's soul or taking the risk of losing the world and gaining one's soul is set before us, the latter is chosen—is risked—less often than it might be.

Still, if the teaching act is directed toward others discovering and claiming their own powers, teachers must take risks. Even more specifically, risk is called for when the powers (as outlined in chapter 5) to be discovered and claimed are not only the powers to receive and to love, but also the powers to rebel, to resist, and to reform. Receptivity and love, yes; rebel, resist, and reform, no—or, at the very most, perhaps. Yet the powers of rebellion, resistance, and reform grow out of receptivity; and if they are exercised humanly, they have a dynamism within them that leads to love.

EXERCISES FOR TAKING RISKS

All five powers are critical for the re-creation and transformation of the world. The following exercises are designed to foster the development of these powers.

Exploring Risk-Takers

Since our courage is often developed from studying and musing on the lives of others, make a list of risk-takers, the risks taken, the tasks accomplished, and the losses incurred. Assign their biographies, suggest that people interview these risk-takers if they are still living, or, if they are deceased, interview people who knew them. See either how many teachers can be listed as risk-takers, or where teaching was a central element in the lives of the risk-takers on the list. See how many risk-takers can be found in the world of art. (The risk-takers need not be famous; part of the exercise can be ferreting out the names of little-known risk-takers, those in one's own family or community.)

Exploring the Outrageous

In order to explore the themes of resistance and rebellion, build a unit with students on the theme, "It's Outrageous" (a suggestion of artist-teacher Deborah Rose). Rose describes the exercise:

The kickoff is a party. Invitations instruct the students (teenagers in this case), to dress outrageously and to bring outrageous tapes of music. The first activity is pair interviews, using questions such as "What is the most outrageous thing you have ever done?" "Who is the most outrageous teacher you have?" "What performing group do you consider totally outrageous?" Dinner consists of build-your-own-tacos, outrageously-gooey cheese nachos, and make-your-own totally outrageous sundaes. During dinner, a rock video provides entertainment— we played part of a "Live-Aid" concert. Any number of outrageous, ridiculous games can be played at such a party, with crazy prizes.

The following week, discussion begins with "What do we mean by outrageous?" The students generate a list of examples. Then they examine the root, or heart of the word, *rage*. Soon everyone begins to see the connections between a Live-Aid concert and outrage against world hunger. From that point on, the group can make lists of things that enrage them. From there they can create a program and projects for an entire year. One possibility for Scripture study would be a discussion such as "Is Christianity Outrageous?" "Was Jesus Christ outrageous?"[25]

And for teachers taking risks, I would add: Are you outrageous? Are you ever outraged? What is the appropriate focus of your rage? To what resistance and reform does it impel you?

Exploring Power

A third exercise, which I was introduced to by Paulo Freire, helps teachers and students explore their own power and uncover powers they might want to develop. Each participant needs at least fifteen minutes to do the following:

- Choose an image, gesture, symbol, book title, or the like that represents your power as a teacher (or student or citizen).
- Tell the others in your group (two or three others seems a good number) what the image is, *and nothing more*.
- For ten minutes, listen to what others see in the image you have chosen; for these ten minutes, you are to be a listener.
- After ten minutes, engage in conversation with your partners, sharing your initial reasons for choosing the symbol, commenting on what they saw that you did not see, and describing any revelation to which their comments have led you about yourself.

I have used this exercise for several years now, and it has proven to be an extraordinary way of discovering powers within. The additional point to include in using it here would be a last question, a final question after discussion:

• What risks will these powers enable you to take?

CONCLUSION

These five criteria (or paths)—taking care, taking steps, taking form, taking time, taking risks—are among those which teachers might look to as they respond to the invitation to bring their own imaginations to bear upon the activity of teaching. The criteria are questions, not answers; suggestions, not demands; counsels, not commandments. Nevertheless, I believe that they have within them much dynamism, much energy, much life. Listen to this ancient prayer to the Creator Spirit, the Divine Source of Imagination:

> Come Holy Spirit,
> Fill the hearts of those who would be faithful,
> Kindle in them the fire of Love.
>
> Send forth your Holy Spirit
> And they shall be created
> And they shall renew the face of the Earth.

I believe the Spirit is waiting to be summoned by teachers who are willing to take care, take steps, take form, take time, and take risks. Outcomes cannot be guaranteed, but the power of imagination is such that if it emerges from our lives, a fire is enkindled and begins to burn. And that fire enables movement in the direction all teaching moves, the direction of re-creation. When re-creation happens, the face of the earth is renewed.

A profound vocation, the vocation to teaching; a profound vocation, the vocation to religious imagination. For it can lead to incarnation, to revelation, and to the grace of power. And these, in turn, can lead to the re-creation of the world.

Notes

INTRODUCTION

1. See Frank Proctor, "Matching Training to a Teacher's Level of Experience," in *Jed Share 13*, 3 (Fall 1982): 20–21. Proctor names Stage I as Survival; Stage II as Basic Competence; Stage III as Broad Experience, and Stage IV as Boredom or Creativity. Although he argues for appropriate teacher instruction for all levels, my study indicates a plethora of materials for Stage I, and a limited number for Stage IV.

2. Among those books directed to teachers who seek a more imaginative and creative role, see Kenneth Eble, *The Craft of Teaching, a Guide to Mastering the Professor's Art* (San Francisco: Jossey-Bass, Higher Education Series, 1976); and Joseph Axelrod, *The University Teacher as Artist: Toward an Aesthetics of Teaching with Emphasis on the Humanities* (San Francisco: Jossey-Bass, 1973).

3. Sylvia Ashton-Warner, *Teacher* (New York: Simon and Schuster, 1963) and *Spearpoint: Teacher in America* (New York: Knopf, 1972); Jonathan Kozol, *Death at an Early Age* (Boston: Houghton Mifflin, 1967); John Holt, *How Children Fail*, rev. ed., orig. 1964 (New York: Delacorte, 1982) and George Dennison, *The Lives of Children* (New York: Random House, 1969); Seonaid Robertson, *Rosegarden and Labyrinth* (London: Routledge & Kegan Paul, 1963); E. R. Braithwaite, *To Sir with Love*, orig. 1973 (New York: New American Library, 1982); Pat Conroy, *The Water Is Wide* (Boston: Houghton Mifflin, 1972); Esther Rothman, *The Angel Inside Went Sour* (New York: David McKay, 1970); Richard Rodriguez, *Hunger of Memory* (Boston: David R. Godine, 1981).

4. See Judy Chicago, *Through the Flower: My Struggles as a Woman* (New York: Doubleday, 1977); and Northrop Frye, *The Great Code* (New York: Harcourt, Brace, Jovanovich, 1981), xi–xxiii.

5. Herman Hesse, *Magister Ludi* (New York: Henry Holt, 1949); *Narcissus and Goldmund* (New York: Bantam Books, 1971); *Siddhartha* (New York: New Directions, 1951).

6. May Sarton, *The Small Room* (New York: W. W. Norton, 1976).

7. James Hilton, *Goodbye, Mr. Chips* (Boston: Little, Brown and Co., 1935).

8. Muriel Spark, *The Prime of Miss Jean Brodie* (Philadelphia: J. B. Lippincott, 1962).

9. See Emlyn Williams, *The Corn is Green* (1938) in *The Collected Plays*, vol. I (New York: Random House, 1961); William Gibson, *The Miracle Worker* (New York: Knopf, 1957); and George Bernard Shaw, *Pygmalion*, in *Bernard Shaw: Selected Plays* (New York: Dodd, Mead and Co., 1981), 511–609.

10. Elliott Landau, Sherrie Epstein, and Ann Stone, eds., *The Teaching Experience: An Introduction to Education Through Literature* (Englewood Cliffs, NJ: Prentice-Hall, 1976).

11. Gilbert Highet, *The Art of Teaching* (New York: Random House, 1954).

12. Paulo Freire, *Pedagogy of the Oppressed* (New York: Herder and Herder, 1970) and *Education for Critical Consciousness* (New York: Seabury, 1973).

13. For R. S. Peters, see *Essays on Educators* (London: Allen & Unwin, 1981); *Ethics and Education* (London: Allen & Unwin, 1966), and *The Concept of Education* (London: Routledge & Kegan Paul, 1970); for John Dewey, see *The Child and the Curriculum* and *The School and Society* (Chicago: University of Chicago Press, 1956) and *Dewey on Education*, selected with Introduction and Notes by Martin Dworkin (New York: Teachers College Press, 1959), especially "My Pedagogic Creed," 19–32.

14. Martin Buber, *Between Man and Man* (London: Kegan Paul, 1947), 83–103.

15. Alfred North Whitehead, *The Aims of Education* (New York: Macmillan, 1929), 15–28.

16. See Maria Montessori, *The Montessori Method*, rev. ed. (New York: Schocken, 1964), as well as her three-volume *Pedagogical Anthropology* (New York: Schocken, 1964).

17. See Elliot Eisner, *The Educational Imagination* (New York: Macmillan, 1979) and *Cognition and Curriculum: A Basis for Deciding What to Teach* (New York: Longman, 1982).

18. See Jane Roland Martin, "Sophie and Emile: A Case Study of Sex Bias in the History of Educational Thought," *Harvard Educational Review 51*, 3 (August 1981): 357–72, and "Excluding Women from the Educational Realm," *Harvard Educational Review 52*, 2 (May 1982): 133–48.

1. IMAGINATION AND THE RELIGIOUS

Epigraph: Wallace Stevens, in "Notes Toward a Supreme Fiction," *The Collected Poems of Wallace Stevens* (New York: Knopf, 1978), 404.

1. Miroslav Holub, "Brief Thoughts on Maps," from *Notes on a Clay Pigeon* (London: Secker and Warburg, 1977), 5. Margaret Woodward brought this poet to my attention.

2. Paul Ricoeur, "The Image of God and the Epic of Man," in *History and Truth* (Evanston, IL: Northwestern University Press, 1965), 127.

3. David Tracy, *The Analogical Imagination* (New York: Crossroad, 1981); Elliot Eisner, *The Educational Imagination* (New York: Macmillan, 1979); Lynn Ross-Bryant, *Imagination and the Life of the Spirit* (Chico, CA: Scholars Press, 1981); John Dixon, *Art and Theological Imagination* (New York: Seabury/Crossroad, 1978); Ray Hart, *Unfinished Man and the Imagination* (Minneapolis: Winston Press, 1979); Walter Brueggemann, *The Prophetic Imagination* (Philadelphia: Fortress Press, 1978).

4. See Gibson Winter, *Liberating Creation: Foundations of Religious Social Ethics* (New York: Crossroad, 1981). Winter suggests, after a careful analysis of metaphors in our Western world, an "artistic paradigm which tilts . . . toward a process of creation and transformation," 128.

5. Adrienne Rich, "When We Dead Awaken: Language as Re-Vision," in *On Lies, Secrets and Silence* (New York: W. W. Norton, 1979), 33–49.

6. Marge Piercy, *The Moon is Always Female* (New York: Knopf, 1981), 17.

7. See Julia Esquivel, *Threatened With Resurrection* (Elgin, IL: The Brethren Press, 1982); Ernesto Cardenal, *Gospel in Solentiname* (Maryknoll: Orbis, 1982 [1979]), and *Psalms* (New York: Crossroad, 1981); see Nadine Gordimer, *July's People* (New York: Viking, 1981) or *Selected Stories* (New York:

Penguin, 1983); see Athol Fugard, *Boesman and Lena and Other Plays* (Oxford: Oxford University Press, 1978) or *A Lesson From Aloes* (Oxford: Oxford University Press, 1981); Paulo Freire, *Pedagogy of the Oppressed* (New York: Herder and Herder, 1970) and *Education for Critical Consciousness* (New York: Seabury, 1973).

8. See Lewis Thomas, *The Lives of a Cell* (New York: Viking, 1974) and *The Medusa and the Snail* (New York: Viking, 1979).

9. See Fritjof Capra, *The Tao of Physics* (New York: Bantam, 1975), 38–39.

10. Paradoxically, imagination can be essentially aim-less; as with all art, it need not be functional, or for use. It can just be.

11. The German word *bildung* is closely related to both art and education. It "clearly indicates the essence of education in the Greek, the Platonic sense; for it covers the artist's act of plastic formation as well as the guiding pattern present to the artist's imagination, the *idea* or *typos*." Werner Jaeger, *Paideia: The Ideals of Greek Culture*, vol. I (New York: Oxford University Press, 1939), xxiii.

12. Coleridge, in the following passage, obviously sees the imagination as closely related to the religious. "The imagination, then, I consider either as primary or secondary. The primary I hold to be the living Power and prime agent of all human perception, and as a repetition in the finite mind of the eternal act of creation in the infinite I AM. The secondary imagination I consider as an echo of the former co-existing with the conscious will, yet still as identical with the primary in the **kind** of its agency, and differing only in **degree** and in the **mode** of its operation. It dissolves, diffuses, dissipates in order to re-create; or where this process is rendered impossible, yet still at all events it struggles to idealize and unify. It is essentially **vital**, even as all objects (**as** objects) are essentially fixed and dead." Samuel Taylor Coleridge, *Biographia Litteraria*, in *Selected Prose and Poetry of Coleridge*, edited by Donald Stauffer (New York: Modern Library, 1951), 263.

13. See Edward S. Casey, *Imagining: A Phenomenological Study* (Bloomington: Indiana University Press, 1976), 3.

14. Coleridge, *Biographia Litteraria*.

15. Samuel Taylor Coleridge, quoted in William Walsh, *Coleridge: The Work and the Relevance* (New York: Barnes and Noble, 1967), 176.

16. William Lynch, *Images of Faith* (Notre Dame: University of Notre Dame Press, 1973), 18–19.

17. *The Variorum Edition of the Poems of W. B. Yeats*, edited by Peter Allt and Russell K. Alspach (New York: The Macmillan Company, 1957), 553.

18. Dwayne Huebner, "Curricular Language and Classroom Meanings," edited by James McDonald and Robert Leeper (Washington, D.C.: ASCD, 1966), 8–26. Reprinted in William Pinar, ed., *Curriculum Theorizing: the Reconceptualists* (Berkeley: McCutchan, 1975), 217–36.

19. Huebner identifies five value frameworks or systems: technical, political, scientific, esthetic, and ethical. See endnote 18, above.

20. Bruce Joyce and Marsha Weil, *Models of Teaching*, 2d ed. (Englewood Cliffs, NJ: Prentice-Hall, 1980). Joyce and Weil call these models "The Personal Sources."

21. Paul Tillich, "Existentialist Aspects of Modern Art," in *Christianity and the Existentialists*, ed. Carl Michelson (New York: Scribner's, 1956), 132.

22. Gabriel Marcel, *Being and Having* (Boston: Beacon, 1951), 27–28.

23. Rudolph Otto, *Idea of the Holy* (New York: Oxford University Press, 1950), 1–40.

24. Nathan Scott, *The Wild Prayer of Longing* (New Haven: Yale University Press, 1971), 49.

25. The Religious Experience Research Unit at Manchester College, Oxford, England, has been studying this phenomenon for several years. See Edward Robinson, *The Original Vision* (New York: Seabury, 1983). See also *Living the Questions*, edited by Edward Robinson (Manchester College, Oxford: Religious Experience Research Unit, 1978) and Timothy Beardsworth, *A Sense of Presence* (Manchester College, Oxford: Religious Experience Research Unit, 1977).

26. T. S. Eliot, "The Dry Salvages" from *Four Quartets* (New York: Harcourt, Brace, Jovanovich, 1971), 44.

27. Harvey Egan, *What Are They Saying About Mysticism?* (New York: Paulist Press, 1982), 1.

28. Walter Stace, *The Teachings of the Mystics* (New York: New American Library, 1960), 14.

29. Thomas Merton wrote in his journal: "There is no way of telling people that they are all walking around shining like the sun." Quoted in Michael Mott, *The Seven Mountains of Thomas Merton* (Boston: Houghton Mifflin, 1984), 312. Nevertheless, such is precisely the mystical apprehension.

30. Philip Wheelwright, *The Burning Fountain* (Gloucester: Peter Smith, 1982). First published 1968.

31. Ibid., 35.

32. Ibid., 38.

33. Edward Bullough, "Psychical Distance as a Factor in Art and an Esthetic Principle," in *A Modern Book of Aesthetics*, edited by Melvin Rader (New York: Henry Holt and Co., 1952). Quoted in Huebner, "Curricular Language," in Pinar, *Curriculum Theorizing*, 235.

34. Wheelwright, *The Burning Fountain*, 50.

35. Freire, *Education for Critical Consciousness*, 96.

36. See Elizabeth Sewell, *The Human Metaphor* (Notre Dame: University of Notre Dame Press, 1964).

2. TEACHING

1. Despite the implied criticism, many of these manuals are helpful not only to beginning teachers, but to more experienced teachers as well. See the series authored by Donald and Patricia Griggs, published by Abingdon Press and the Instroteach Program of Scottsdale, Arizona. See the work of Richard Curwin and Barbara Fuhrmann, *Discovering Your Teaching Self* (Englewood Cliffs, NJ: Prentice-Hall, 1976) and Thomas Gordon, *Teacher Effectiveness Training* (New York: Peter Wyden, 1972).

2. William Walsh, *The Use of Imagination: Educational Thought and the Literary Mind* (New York: Barnes and Noble, 1960), 64.

3. For this rendering of the meaning of steps, I am indebted to Judith Dorney.

4. I distinguish here between the word *contemplative* used as a quality or characteristic in the first chapter to specify a particular way in which imagination operates, and *contemplation* as a direct and dynamic activity in itself. The two, although related, are also distinct.

5. Gerald May, *Will and Spirit: A Contemplative Psychology* (San Francisco: Harper & Row, 1982), 25.

6. Annie Dillard, *Pilgrim at Tinker Creek* (New York: Bantam, 1974), 15–16.

7. This human presence is one of the arguments against machines replacing people as teachers.
8. May Sarton, *The Small Room* (New York: W. W. Norton, 1976), 217.
9. Elliot Eisner, *The Educational Imagination* (New York: Macmillan, 1979), 74 ff.
10. Ben Shahn, *The Shape of Content* (New York: Vintage, 1957), 17–29.
11. James Worley, "Mark Van Doren (1946)," in *Christian Century XCVI*, 33 (October 17, 1979): 1006.
12. Walsh, *The Use of Imagination*, 55–56.
13. See Paulo Freire, *Pedagogy of the Oppressed* (New York: Herder and Herder, 1970), 12–13, 20 ff.
14. It is important to note this Subjectivity is not a fourth in a series of Subjects, but in and of and over and through; a kind of circumincession throughout all other subjectivity.
15. Martin Buber, *Between Man and Man* (London: Kegan Paul, 1947), 103.
16. Ibid., 99.
17. Ibid., 100.
18. Walsh, *The Use of Imagination*, 36.
19. Helen Keller, *Story of My Life* (Garden City, NY: Doubleday, 1936), 23–24.
20. Quoted in Eisner, *The Educational Imagination*, 74.
21. Nikos Kazantzakis, *Zorba the Greek* (New York: Simon and Schuster, 1952), 120–21.
22. See Gabriel Moran, *Religious Body* (New York: Seabury, 1974), 162–63.
23. Par Lagerkvist in *Evening Land/Aftonland*, translated by W. H. Auden and Leif Sjöberg, orig. 1953 (London: Souvenir Press, 1977), 141.

3. INCARNATION

1. Ben Shahn, *The Shape of Content* (New York: Vintage, 1957), 81.
2. Mary Boys, "Access to Traditions and Transformation," in *Transformation and Tradition in Religious Education*, edited by Padraic O'Hare (Birmingham: Religious Education Press, 1979), 9–34.
3. See David A. Kolb and Ronald Fry, "Towards an Applied Theory of Experiential Learning," in *Theories of Group Process*, edited by Cary Cooper (New York: John Wiley and Sons, 1975), 33 ff.
4. Elizabeth Sewell, *The Human Metaphor* (Notre Dame: University of Notre Dame Press, 1964), 37. (Note: Sewell cites the Blake poem.)
5. Philip Wheelwright, *The Burning Fountain* (Gloucester: Peter Smith, 1982), 3–4, 73–101. Wheelwright is at pains to point out that the differentiation is by no means absolute, but basically that steno-language is literal language in black and white, whereas expressive language is poetic, manifold, paradoxical language in color of every shade and fullness.
6. Suzanne Langer, *Philosophy in a New Key*, 3d ed., orig. 1942 (Cambridge: Harvard University Press, 1969). Note especially chapter 4, "Discursive Forms and Presentational Forms," 79–102. Discursive form is generally in the shape of discourse: linear and translatable. Presentational form, although at times verbal—in drama, novel, poetry—is usually in the shape of art: all-at-once, rather than sequential, and susceptible to multiple interpretations.
7. See William J. J. Gordon, *Synectics* (New York: Harper & Row, 1961); George M. Prince, *The Practice of Creativity* (New York: Harper & Row, 1970).

8. Robert Samples, *The Metaphoric Mind* (Reading: Addison Wesley, 1976), 91.
9. Ira Progoff, *At a Journal Workshop* (New York: Dialogue House Library, 1975).
10. Prince, *Creativity*, 80.
11. Rosemary Radford Ruether, *Journeys*, edited by Gregory Baum (New York: Paulist, 1975), 41.
12. Carlos Casteneda, *A Separate Reality: Further Conversations with Don Juan* (New York: Simon and Schuster, 1971), 4.
13. Naum Gabo, in Brenda Lealman and Edward Robinson, *The Image of Life* (Oxford: Religious Experience Research United and CEM Press, 1980), 13–14.
14. Chief Seattle, in *A.D. 9*, 5 (May 1980): 30–31. How different is this spirituality from one that proposes "contempt for the world."
15. Dorothea Soelle, *Death by Bread Alone* (Philadelphia: Fortress, 1978), 138.
16. Samples, *The Metaphoric Mind*, 92 ff.
17. Delia Ephron, *How to Eat Like a Child and Other Lessons in Not Being a Grownup* (New York: Viking, 1978), 1–5.
18. Abraham Joshua Heschel, *The Prophets*, vol. 1, orig. 1955 (New York: Harper & Row, 1962), xi.

4. REVELATION

1. Abraham Joshua Heschel, *The Prophets*, vol. 1 (New York: Harper & Row, 1962), xi.
2. See Gabriel Moran, *Theology of Revelation* (New York: Herder and Herder, 1966), *Catechesis of Revelation* (New York: Herder and Herder, 1966), and *The Present Revelation* (New York: Herder and Herder, 1972).
3. Gabriel Moran, "Revelation and Community," in Gabriel Moran and Maria Harris, *Experiences in Community* (New York: Herder and Herder, 1968), 75.
4. Ibid.
5. Jerome Bruner, *On Knowing* (Cambridge: Belknap Press of Harvard University, 1962), 82–83. What Bruner calls rearranging and transforming evidence, I call incarnation; what he calls going beyond the evidence to new insights, I call revelation.
6. Northrop Frye, *The Great Code* (New York: Harcourt, Brace, Jovanovich, 1981), xv.
7. Roger Hazelton, *Ascending Flame, Descending Dove* (Philadelphia: Westminster, 1975), 64.
8. Ibid., 64–65.
9. Ibid., 65.
10. William Walsh, *The Use of Imagination: Educational Thought and the Literary Mind* (New York: Barnes and Noble, 1960), 65.
11. Sara Little, *To Set One's Heart* (Atlanta: John Knox, 1983), 59–60.
12. James D. Whitehill, "The Indirect Communication: Kierkegaard and Beckett," in *Art and Religion as Communication*, edited by James Waddell and F. W. Dillistone (Atlanta: John Knox, 1974), 79–93. See also Edward Robinson, "Loneliness and Communication," in *Theology LXXXIII*, 693 (May 1980): 195–203. For Kierkegaard's text, see Sören Kierkegaard, *Concluding Unscientific Postscript*, translated from the Danish by David Swenson; Introduction by Walter Lowrie, orig. 1941. (Princeton, NJ: Princeton University Press, 1968).

13. Martin Buber, *Between Man and Man* (London: Kegan Paul, 1947), 90.
14. Sylvia Ashton-Warner, *Teacher* (New York: Simon and Schuster, 1963).
15. Seonaid Robertson, *Rosegarden and Labyrinth* (London: Routledge & Kegan Paul, 1963), 107.
16. Paulo Freire, *Education for Critical Consciousness* (New York: Seabury, 1973).
17. Buber, *Between Man and Man*, 110.
18. From Theodore Roethke, "How Can I Dream Except Beyond This Life?" from "The Abyss," in *Collected Poems* (London: Faber, 1968), 189.
19. Whitehill, "The Indirect Communication," *Art and Religion*, 83.
20. Wheelwright, *The Burning Fountain*, 84–96.
21. Little, *To Set One's Heart*, 61.
22. Kierkegaard, quoted in Whitehill, "The Indirect Communication," *Art and Religion*, 83.
23. Gloria T. Hull, Patricia Bell Scott, and Barbara Smith, *All the Women Are White, All the Blacks Are Men, But Some of Us Are Brave* (Old Westbury, NY: The Feminist Press, 1982).
24. Alice Walker, *The Color Purple* (New York: Washington Square Press, 1982), 247.
25. Thomas Merton, in Michael Mott, *The Seven Mountains of Thomas Merton* (Boston: Houghton Mifflin, 1984), 300–301.
26. Buber, *Between Man and Man*, 102.
27. Judy Chicago, *The Dinner Party* (New York: Doubleday, 1979), 256.

5. THE GRACE OF POWER

1. Edward Robinson, "Education and Unreality," in *Learning for Living* (previous title of *British Journal of Religious Education*) (1977): 166–67.
2. The power revealed is not, however, granted or given from outside the person; it is instead a discovery of power within the living subject, who comes to know her or his own capacities as already possessed and now becoming active and activated.
3. Jurgen Habermas, "Hannah Arendt: On the Concept of Power," in *Philosophical and Political Profiles*, translated by Frederick Lawrence (Cambridge, MA: MIT Press, 1983), 171.
4. Rollo May, *Power and Innocence* (New York: Norton, 1972).
5. Talcott Parsons, "On the Concept of Power," in *Sociological Theory and Modern Society* (New York: 1967), 310 ff.
6. Elizabeth Janeway, *Powers of the Weak* (New York: Knopf, 1980), 157; 161–85.
7. Jean Johnson, in an unpublished lecture, New York University, Program in Religious Education, July 8, 1982.
8. Margaret Atwood, *Surfacing* (New York: Simon and Schuster, 1972), 222–23.
9. Johannes Baptist Metz, *Theology of the World*, translated by William Glen Doepel (New York: Herder and Herder, 1971), 107.
10. Ntozake Shange, *for colored girls who have considered suicide when the rainbow is enuf* (New York: Macmillan, 1977), 66.
11. See Dwayne Huebner, "Curricular Language and Classroom Meanings," in William Pinar, ed., *Curriculum Theorizing: The Reconceptualists* (Berkeley: McCutchan, 1975), 222.
12. See Elliot Eisner, *The Educational Imagination* (New York: Macmillan, 1979), 50–73.
13. Ibid., 70.

14. Ibid. See also Elliot Eisner and Elizabeth Vallance, eds., *Conflicting Conceptions of Curriculum* (Berkeley: McCutchan, 1974).
15. Paulo Freire, *Education for Critical Consciousness* (New York: Seabury, 1973), 48.
16. Gabriel Moran, *Education Toward Adulthood* (New York: Paulist Press, 1979), *Interplay* (Winona, MN: St. Mary's Press, 1981), and *Religious Education Development* (Minneapolis: Winston Press, 1983).
17. Moran, "A Grammar of Educational Development," in *Religious Education Development*, 157–82.
18. Constance Urdang, "Living in the Third World," in *The American Poetry Review* (March/April 1977) vol. 6, #2.
19. For examples of such philosophers in action, see Pinar, *Curriculum Theorizing*, 87 ff. See especially the analysis and suggestions made by Michael Apple in "The Hidden Curriculum and the Nature of Conflict," in Pinar, 95–119.
20. In Huebner, "The Tasks of the Curricular Theorist," in Pinar, *Curriculum Theorizing*, 276 ff.
21. Ibid.
22. James Douglass, *Lightning East and West* (Portland: Sunburst Press, 1981), 74.
23. John Fry, *The Great Apostolic Blunder Machine* (New York: Harper & Row, 1978), 74–75.
24. Albert Camus, *The Rebel*, orig. 1956 (New York: Knopf, 1967), 28.
25. Freire, *Education for Critical Consciousness*, 35–36.
26. Ibid., 10–11.
27. Ibid., 97.
28. See Maria Harris, *Portrait of Youth Ministry* (New York: Paulist Press, 1981), 149–53.
29. John C. Raines, "Righteous Resistance and Martin Luther King," in *Christian Century* (January 1, 1984): 53.
30. Thomas S. Kuhn, *The Structure of Scientific Revolutions* (Chicago: University of Chicago Press, 1973 [orig. 1962]), 91–92.

6. RE-CREATION

1. Paulo Freire, *Pedagogy of the Oppressed* (New York: Herder and Herder, 1970), 86 ff.
2. Catherina Halkes, "Feminist Theology: An Interim Assessment," in *Women in a Man's Church*, edited by Virgil Elizondo and Norbert Greinacher (Minneapolis: Seabury/Winston, New Concilium Series, vol. 134: 1980), 120–21.
3. Ibid.
4. Elliot Eisner, *The Educational Imagination* (New York: Macmillan, 1979). See chapter 5, 74–92.
5. Ibid., 153.
6. Tillie Olsen, *Silences* (New York: Dell, 1979); Adrienne Rich, *On Lies, Secrets and Silence* (New York: W. W. Norton, 1979); Nancy A. Falk and Rita M. Gross, eds., *Unspoken Worlds: Women's Religious Lives in Non-Western Cultures* (San Francisco: Harper & Row, 1980); Carol Gilligan, *In a Different Voice: Psychological Theory and Women's Development* (Harvard: Cambridge University Press, 1982).

7. See "The Human Situation: A Feminine View," in *Womanspirit Rising,* edited by Carol Christ and Judith Plaskow (New York: Harper & Row, 1979), 29–42 (Orig. 1960 in *The Journal of Religion* (April 1960), © University of Chicago Press.)

8. See Mary Daly, *Gyn/Ecology: The Metaethics of Radical Feminism* (Boston: Beacon, 1978) and Andrea Dworkin, *Woman Hating: A Radical Look at Sexuality* (New York: E. P. Dutton, 1976), for further development of these ideas.

9. See Barbara Wheeler, "Accountability to Women in Theological Seminaries," in *Religious Education 76,* 4 (July–August 1981): 390.

10. *Pintig: Lifepulse in Cold Steel* (Kowloon, Hong Kong: Resource Center for Philippine Concerns, 1979), 118.

11. See Judith Dorney, "The Working Class Woman: Her Challenge to Religious Education," in *Religious Education 79,* 2 (Spring 1984): 229–42 and "The Religious Education of Young Women" in *Women's Issues in Religious Education,* edited by Fern Giltner (Birmingham: Religious Education Press, 1985).

12. Quoted by Susan Griffin in *Rape: The Power of Consciousness* (New York: Harper & Row, 1979), 42.

13. Martin Buber, *Between Man and Man* (London: Kegan Paul, 1947), 8–11.

14. Albert Camus, *The Rebel,* orig. 1956 (New York: Knopf), 28.

15. Ibid.

16. See Brian Wren, *Education for Justice* (Maryknoll: Orbis, 1977), 12 ff.; and Paulo Freire, *Education for Critical Consciousness* (New York: Seabury, 1973).

17. James McGinnis, et al. *Educating for Peace and Justice: Religious Dimensions* (St. Louis: Institute for Peace and Justice, 1984), 145.

18. Virginia Woolf, *Three Guineas,* orig. 1938 (New York: Harcourt, Brace, Jovanovich, 1966), 80 ff.

19. Ibid.

20. John Keats, "Hyperion," in Book III of *The Complete Poetical Works of Keats* (Boston: Houghton Mifflin, Cambridge Edition, 1899), 8th printing, 211–12.

21. Erich Lindemann, "Symptomatology and Management of Acute Grief," in Robert Fulton, ed., *Death and Identity* (New York: John Wiley and Sons, Inc., 1965), 186–201. Reprinted from *American Journal of Psychiatry 101* (1944): 141–48.

22. See Elisabeth Kübler-Ross, *On Death and Dying* (New York: Macmillan, 1969).

23. See Beverly Harrison's inaugural lecture, "The Power of Anger in the Work of Love: Christian Ethics for Women and Other Strangers," in *Union Theological Seminary Review* (Supplementary, 1981): 41–57.

24. See Daniel Maguire, "Abortion: A Question of Catholic Honesty," in *The Christian Century* (September 14–21, 1983): 807.

25. Judy Collins, "Bread and Roses," on *The First Fifteen Years* (Los Angeles: Elektra/Asylum Records, 1977).

26. "Singing For Our Lives," recorded by Holly Near and Ronnie Gilbert on *Lifeline* (Oakland: Redwood Records, 1983).

27. "Sister" recorded by Cris Williamson on *The Changer and the Changed* (Oakland: Olivia Records, 1975).

28. In Jane Austen, *Pride and Prejudice* (New York: Bantam, 1981).

29. In Alice Walker, *The Color Purple* (New York: Washington Square Press, 1982).

30. In Mary Gordon, *Final Payments* (New York: Random House, 1978).

31. Louisa May Alcott, *Little Women* (Boston: Little, Brown, 1968, Centennial Edition).

32. See Judith Plaskow Goldenberg with Karen Bloomquist, Margaret Early and Elizabeth Farians, "Epilogue: The Coming of Lilith," in *Religion and Sexism*, edited by Rosemary Radford Ruether (New York: Simon and Schuster, 1974), 341–43.

33. See Luke 1.

34. See Phyllis Trible, *God and the Rhetoric of Sexuality* (Philadelphia: Fortress, 1978), 166–99.

35. Jean Johnson, in an unpublished lecture, July 8, 1982.

36. Sophia Lyon Fahs, *Today's Children and Yesterday's Heritage* (Boston: Beacon, 1952), 114. See also chapter 8, "Old and New Cosmologies," 101–23.

37. Charlotte Perkins Gilman, quoted in Rosemary Radford Ruether, *Sexism and God-Talk* (Boston: Beacon, 1983), 236.

38. *The Corn is Green* in *Emlyn Williams: The Collected Plays*, vol. 1, orig. 1938 (New York: Random House, 1961), 263.

39. Quoted in Matthew Fox, *Original Blessing: A Primer in Creation Spirituality* (Santa Fe: Bear and Co., 1983), 222.

40. Judy Chicago, *The Dinner Party* (New York: Doubleday, 1979), 256.

7. A PEDAGOGICAL MODEL

1. Philip Jackson, *Life in Classrooms* (New York: Holt, Rinehart and Winston, 1968), 115.

2. John Dewey, *The Sources of a Science of Education* (New York: Liveright, 1929), 10–11.

3. I define pedagogy here as knowledge about teaching. I would emphasize the fact, however, that I take knowledge to mean the sum of bodily, human, and receptive characteristics essential to human understanding; and I take knowing to be an embodied human activity, as opposed to a concept of knowledge as a product of intelligence or as the equivalent of explicit judgments of the mind. "Knowledge which is meaningful is not merely cerebral. Genuine knowledge involves the viscera, the muscles and the glands." See Nathaniel Cantor, *The Teaching-Learning Process* (New York: The Dryden Press, 1953), 70.

4. It would be misleading to suggest that this style of teaching did not include input from books as well. One discussion class, for example, was spent on our reactions to the book that helped put so many of my aesthetic and educational questions into perspective, John Dewey's *Art As Experience* (New York: G. P. Putnam's Sons, 1934).

5. B. Othanel Smith, "On the Anatomy of Teaching," in the *Journal of Teacher Education VII*, 4 (December 1956): 342.

6. Mary Jane Aschner, "The Language of Teaching," in B. Smith and Robert Ennis, eds., *Language and Concepts in Education* (Chicago: Rand McNally, 1961), 112.

7. Abraham Shumsky, *In Search of Teaching Style* (New York: Appleton-Century-Crofts, 1968), 84.

8. See Dewey, *Art as Experience*.

9. Dwayne Huebner, "Curricular Language and Classroom Meanings," in William Pinar, ed., *Curriculum Theorizing: the Reconceptualists* (Berkeley: McCutchan, 1975).

10. See especially Ernst Cassirer, *An Essay on Man* (New Haven: Yale University Press, 1944).
11. See especially the following books by Suzanne Langer: *Feeling and Form* (New York: Charles Scribner's Sons, 1953); *Mind: An Essay on Human Feeling*, vol. I (Baltimore: Johns Hopkins Press, 1967); *Problems of Art* (New York: Charles Scribner's Sons, 1957); and (ed.) *Reflections on Art* (Baltimore: Johns Hopkins Press, 1958).
12. This and all subsequent direct quotations of Mary Tully are taken either from my notes or from audio tapes of our classes and conversations from September 1969 through January 1970.
13. This quote is attributed to William James, without citation, by Dewey in *Art as Experience*, 72.
14. Paul Tillich, *Theology of Culture* (New York: Oxford University Press, 1959), 75.
15. Dewey, *Art As Experience*, 15.
16. Ibid., 38.

8. AN ARTISTIC MODEL

Epigraph: This and other student comments quoted throughout this chapter are taken from the final papers I requested from each student in the course "The Aesthetic and Religious Education." In the year from which this quote is taken, I had asked the students to respond to three questions: (1) What was your contribution to the course? (2) What was the course's contribution to you? (3) How would you explain the relations between the aesthetic, education, and the religious? Diane Lockwood's poem is her response to question two.

1. Catalog description of the course, "The Aesthetic and Religious Education."
2. See chapter 7, note 11.
3. See John Dewey, *Democracy and Education* (New York: Macmillan, 1916). He speaks of education (on page 76) as "that reconstruction or reorganization of experience, which adds to the meaning of experience, and which increases ability to direct the course of subsequent experience." Note especially Dewey's emphasis on reforming and reshaping, or, using his metaphors, reorganizing and reconstructing.
4. See for example, Erik Erikson, *Childhood and Society* (New York: W. W. Norton, 1950); James Fowler, *Stages of Faith* (San Francisco: Harper & Row, 1981); Jean Piaget, *Genetic Epistemology* (New York: Columbia University Press, 1970); and Lawrence Kohlberg, *The Philosophy of Moral Development* (San Francisco: Harper & Row, 1981).
5. Howard Gardner, *The Arts and Human Development* (New York: John Wiley and Sons, 1973), vi.
6. See Jean Baker Miller, *Toward a New Psychology of Women* (Boston: Beacon, 1976), 94.
7. See the following books by Lewis Thomas: *The Lives of a Cell: Notes of a Biology Watcher* (New York: Viking, 1974); *The Medusa and the Snail* (New York: Viking, 1979); and *The Youngest Science: Notes of a Medicine Watcher* (New York: Viking, 1983).
8. Fritjof Capra, *The Tao of Physics* (New York: Bantam, 1975), 233.
9. Dewey, *Art as Experience*, 73.
10. Ibid.
11. Mary Anderson Tully, in a personal interview, December 9, 1969.

12. See note 1, above.
13. See Gardner, *The Arts and Human Development*, for an elaboration of these roles.
14. See note 1, above.
15. See Suzanne Langer, *Philosophy in a New Key*, 3d ed., orig. 1942 (Cambridge: Harvard University Press, 1969), especially note 6, chapter 3.
16. See note 1, above.
17. The phrase, although simple, appears to have a powerful effect on students in helping them through initial fears. In time, students come to believe it, at least in this situation.
18. See note 1, above.
19. See Jerome Bruner, *On Knowing* (Cambridge: Belknap Press of Harvard University, 1962). According to Bruner, these qualities are "the conditions of creativity." See pp. 23 ff.
20. See note 1, above.
21. Ibid.

9. INVITATION TO IMAGINATION

1. See Thich Nhat Hanh, *The Miracle of Mindfulness* (Boston: Beacon Press, 1976).
2. See Mary Terese Donze, *In My Heart Room* (Liguori, MO: Liguori Publications, 1982) for examples of such exercises with children.
3. See Maria Harris, *The D.R.E. Book* (New York: Paulist Press, 1976) for further commentary on the Myth of Care, drawn from the work of philosopher Martin Heidegger.
4. For elaboration on this exercise, and for similar exercises, see the teacher's guide to the videotape program "Teaching and Religious Imagination," by Maria Harris (Allen, Tex.: Argus Communications, 1985).
5. See Alfred North Whitehead, *The Aims of Education* (New York: Macmillan, 1929), chapter 2, "The Rhythm of Education."
6. See chapter 6, above, p. 000. See also note 16, below.
7. Alice Walker, *The Color Purple* (New York: Washington Square Press, 1982).
8. Examples of such rituals can be found in Franklin Littell, *The Crucifixion of the Jews* (New York: Harper & Row, 1975), 141–53. See also Eugene J. Fisher and Leon Klenicki, *From Death to Hope: Liturgical Reflections on the Holocaust* (New York: Anti-Defamation League of B'nai Brith, 1985).
9. See William Bean Kennedy, "Christian Education and Mission into the Twenty-First Century," in *Theodolite* 7, 6 (1986): 8.
10. See the following books by Kenneth Koch: *Wishes, Lies and Dreams: Teaching Children to Write Poetry* (New York: Random House, 1970); *I Never Told Anybody: Teaching Poetry Writing in a Nursing Home* (New York: Random House, 1970); and *Rose, Where Did You Get That Red?* (New York: Vintage, 1974).
11. Rupert Brooke, "The Soldier," in Oscar Williams, ed., *The War Poets* (New York: John Day Co., 1945), 48.
12. Wilfred Owen, "Dulce et Decorum Est," in Brooke, *The New Poets*, 37–38.
13. Koch, *Wishes, Lies and Dreams* and *I Never Told Anybody*.
14. Paddy Chayefsky, *Gideon* (New York: Random House, 1961), 54.
15. Robert Graves, "In Broken Images," in *Collected Poems* (London: Cassell, 1975), 80.

16. Rainer Maria Rilke, *Letters to a Young Poet* (New York: W. W. Norton, 1934), 33.

17. See Francis Hunkins, *Involving Students in Questioning* (Boston: Allyn and Bacon, 1976) and *Questioning Strategies and Techniques* (Boston: Allyn and Bacon, 1972).

18. See Maria Harris, "Enlarging the Religious Imagination: The Imagery of Time," in *PACE 13* (Winona, MN.: St. Mary's Press, 1982–1983), Issue F: 1–4.

19. Lawrence Cremin, *Public Education* (New York: Basic Books, 1976), 27. For a systematic and careful critique of this definition and for an alternative model, see Gabriel Moran, *Interplay: A Theory of Religion and Education* (Winona, MN: St. Mary's Press, 1981), especially chapter 3.

20. Jamake Highwater, *The Primal Mind: Vision and Reality in Indian America* (New York: Harper & Row, 1981), 81.

21. Gibson Winter, *Liberating Creation: Foundations of Religious Social Ethics* (New York: Crossroad, 1981), 1.

22. Highwater, *Primal Mind*, 105.

23. See Annie Dillard, *Living by Fiction* (New York: Harper & Row, 1982), 20 ff.

24. Samuel Terrien, *The Elusive Presence: Toward a New Biblical Theology* (San Francisco: Harper & Row, 1978), 393.

25. Deborah Rose, in an unpublished paper (Newton, MA: Andover Newton Theological School, December 1985).

Index

ACKNOWLEDGMENTS:

Rupert Brooke, "The Soldier," from *The Collected Poems of Rupert Brooke.* Reprinted by permission of Dodd, Mead and Company, Inc. Copyright © 1915 by Dodd, Mead and Company. Copyright renewed 1943 by Edward Marsh.

Paddy Chayefsky, *Gideon.* Copyright © 1961. Reprinted by permission of Random House, Inc.

Judy Chicago, from *The Dinner Party.* Copyright © 1979 by Judy Chicago. Reprinted by permission of Doubleday & Company, Inc.

Annie Dillard, *Pilgrim at Tinker Creek.* Copyright © 1974 by Annie Dillard. Reprinted by permission of Harper & Row, Publishers, Inc.

James Douglass, *Lightning East to West.* Sunburst Press, 1980 edition. Copyright © James Douglass. Reprinted with permission of the author, by permission of Sunburst Press, and by permission of The Crossroad Publishing Company (1983 edition).

Gloria Durka and Joanmarie Smith, editors, *The Aesthetic Dimension of Religious Education* for permission to reprint a revised version of "A Model for Aesthetic Education." Copyright © 1979, Gloria Durka and Joanmarie Smith, 1979. Also by permission of Paulist Press.

T. S. Eliot from "The Dry Salvages," in *Four Quartets.* Copyright 1943 by T. S. Eliot; renewed 1971 by Esme Valerie Eliot. Reprinted by permission of Harcourt Brace Jovanovich, Inc.

Robert Graves, "In Broken Images" from *Collected Poems 1975.* Reprinted by permission of A. P. Watt Ltd. on behalf of the executors of the Estate of Robert Graves © Robert Graves and by permission of Oxford University Press, New York.

Roger Hazelton, *Ascending Flame, Descending Dove.* Copyright © 1975 The Westminster Press. Reprinted and used by permission.

Francis P. Hunkins. Material adapted from Francis P. Hunkins, *Questioning Strategies and Techniques,* 1972 and Francis P. Hunkins, *Involving Students in Questioning,* 1976, originally published by Allyn and Bacon. Used by permission of Francis P. Hunkins.

Par Lagerkvist, from *Evening Land/Aftonland.* Reprinted from *Prism International,* Vol. 12/2, Summer 1972. With permission.

Thomas Merton, from *Raids on the Unspeakable.* Copyright © 1966 by the Abbey of Gethsemani, Inc. Reprinted by permission of New Directions Publishing Coporation and Laurence Polligner Ltd. Search Press Ltd.

Wilfred Owen, "Dulce et Decorum Est," from *Collected Poems*. Copyright © 1963 by Chatto & Windus Ltd. Permission of New Directions Publishing Corporation.

Theodore Roethke, "The Abyss" from *The Collected Poems of Theodore Roethke* copyright © 1963 by Beatrice Roethke as administratrix of the Estate of Theodore Roethke. Reprinted by permission of Doubleday & Company, Inc. and Faber and Faber Ltd.

Constance Urdang, "Living in the Third World," with permission of the author. First appeared in *The American Poetry Review*.

William Walsh, *The Use of Imagination*. Reprinted by permission of Chatto & Windus: The Hogarth Press Ltd. and Barnes and Noble Books.

James Worley, "Mark Van Doren." Copyright © Christian Century Foundation. Reprinted by permission from the October 17, 1979 issue of The Christian Century.

And to Marcia Dorey, Thomas Evans, Bill Maroon, Diane Lockwood Wendorf, and Deborah Rose for permission to print original material.